Reading passages and dialogs:
MP3 free download

중급교양영어

Freshman English 2

Second Edition

Andrew Finch

KNU PRESS

Author: Dr. Andrew Finch is Professor of English Education in the Teachers' College of Kyungpook National University, where he teaches graduate and undergraduate pre-service and in-service teachers of English. His courses and teacher training seminars include Teaching Methodology, Classroom-based Assessment, Drama in ELT, Multimedia, Materials Design, and Qualitative Research methods. In addition to more than 20 years in Korea, Dr. Finch has worked in Hong Kong as a testing consultant and has authored various books, international articles, EFL programs and textbooks, and English discussion books. He was visiting research fellow at the Graduate School of Education (TESOL), Bristol University, UK, during his sabbatical year, and his Ph.D. (Manchester University, UK) was on language program assessment. Dr. Finch loves Baduk, hiking, and Cheonggukjang.

Editor and Drama Project Advisor: Dr. Heebon Park is Assistant Professor in the College of Liberal Education of Keimyung University. She has a Ph.D. in Modern British Drama from Bristol University, UK, and a Ph.D. in English Literature from Kyungpook National University. Dr. Park was a visiting scholar at UC Berkeley and has written English TV program scripts for Daegu MBC, in addition to her experience as International Coordinator and Official Interpreter for the Gyeongju World Culture EXPO Organizing Committee.

MP3 Recording: Graham Beals, Kirsty Clausen, Vincent Greenier, Dr. Dieter Knowle, Kenneth Quillinan, Lowell Sanborn.

중급교양영어
Freshman English 2

First edition published 11 June 2012
Second edition published 8 August 2013

Published by Kyungpook National University Press

Address | 80 Daehak-ro, Buk-gu, Daegu, Korea
Tel | (+82) 53-950-6741~3 Fax | (+82) 53-953-4692
E-mail | press@knu.ac.kr Website | http://press.knu.ac.kr

ISBN 978-89-7180-378-3 13740

Foreword

Welcome to the second edition of **Freshman English 2**. This book helps students to acquire the spoken and written English needed for their studies and their careers. Building upon the student-centered, task-based content of **Freshman English 1**, this book shows students how to write their own short bios, résumés, cover letters, personal statements, and reviews, in addition to learning spoken interview skills. These job-based topics provide a strong foundation in practical and professional English.

Creativity, collaboration, performance, and presentation, are at the heart of **Freshman English 2**, which encourages students to become actively involved in their learning, particularly in the final Units, when they produce a drama project and a print media project. These speaking/writing projects allow them to develop social skills as well as affective, cognitive, and linguistic skills. This holistic, whole-person approach is important for future professionals, since language use involves personality, culture, society, and relationship.

Input is important in language learning, and this is supplied in the **Word Bank** at the back of this book, where vocabulary and functional phrases provide students of every level with the language they need, along with answers to the various puzzles in the book and a glossary of key words. There are also many opportunities for output throughout the book, presenting learners with a balanced approach to the complex task of acquiring and using meaningful language.

Confidence, motivation, and a positive attitude are also extremely important. For this reason, **Freshman English 2** promotes a non-threatening, cooperative learning environment. Learning English is not a competition; there need be no winners or losers. Students have their own individual learning styles and should be allowed to learn English in the way that is best for them. Motivation, confidence, self-esteem, and ongoing learning (growth) are most important, irrespective of the level of proficiency.

English language teaching and learning are experiencing great changes at this time. The Internet is revolutionizing the way people learn, and smart technology is changing the way we communicate. Teachers and learners need to make the most of these new opportunities, and the website at www.finchpark.com/KNUFLE, which was specially designed for this series, helps them to achieve that goal, with its various e-learning links and resources.

Finally, I wish to express my thanks and appreciation to the KNU executives who made this program possible, members of KNU press for their active support, and all the teachers who offered their invaluable feedback on the first edition, thereby helping this book to grow into its present form. I also thank professor Kim No-Ju for suggesting the Language Workshop topics, as well as the proofreaders, who contributed their time and valuable insights, and the Freshman English teaching staff who recorded the reading passages and dialogs. My sincere hope is that this book will provide an enjoyable, challenging, and fruitful learning experience for all its users.

Andrew Finch
June 2013

How to use this book (1)

Introduction

Freshman English 2 is the second book in the series and builds upon the holistic, task-based, student-centered foundation of **Freshman English 1**. Continuing the process of learning that focused on conversation skills and paragraph writing in the earlier book, **Freshman English 2** helps students apply these skills in a career-oriented direction, providing the theory and practice that they will need when applying for jobs and when employed in a bilingual working environment.

Freshman English 2 begins by reviewing the learning from **Freshman English 1** and exploring the personalities of the students (Unit 1), before helping them acquire various academic English skills (Units 1 to 8). Units 9 and 10 then complete the series by inviting students to design and perform a speaking project (Unit 9, Drama) and a writing project (Unit 10, Print Media).

Units 1 to 8 thus have a professional focus: 1) Application forms; 2) Short bios; 3) Résumés; 4) Autobiographies; 5) Interviews and follow-up emails; 6) Personal statements; 7) Cover letters; and 8) reviews. Units 9 and 10 can be seen as the culmination of everything that has been studied in Books 1 and 2. These final Units offer students an extra opportunity to demonstrate their creativity and teamwork, before closing this chapter on their learning paths.

Each Unit in **Freshman English 2** takes an integrated approach, though Units 1 to 8 can be divided into two sections - oral and written production (**Part 1** and **Part 2**). However, teachers and learners should feel free to study the content in ways that are appropriate for them. It is not necessary for every student to perform every activity, or for every student to be working on the same activity at the same time. It is more effective to look upon activities as affordances, providing different learning opportunities for different students.

Flexibility and suitability are key words. Advanced level students might wish to work on the more difficult activities or spend longer on writing, producing lengthier and more polished output. On the other hand, basic level students might want to focus on simpler activities, along with the vocabulary and phrases in the Word Bank. As long as everyone produces written output in the final pages of each Unit, it should be possible to have a multi-level classroom in which everyone is working on speaking and writing tasks appropriate for their level of proficiency.

Units 1 to 8, Part 1 (oral production)

The first page of each Unit introduces students to the theme and content of the Unit. This is an individual, awareness-raising activity, which is then discussed in pairs. It is followed either by a reading and discussion activity or a 'Campus Friends' episode, in which the lives of six friends are followed as they apply to be reporters on the University English newspaper. Their experiences mirror, clarify, and supplement the content of each Unit. The reading/discussion pages offer linguistic input and are formatted as print media. This familiarizes students with the form and content of print media, in preparation for Unit 10. Other activities in Part 1 develop the theme of the Unit in an interactive manner.

How to use this book (2)

Units 1 to 8, Part 2 (written production)

The writing goals of the book are addressed in the second half of each of these Units. Using a process-writing approach, students write a first draft of their bio, résumé, personal statement, etc., have this peer-edited by a classmate, and then write a final draft, which is placed in the portfolio pocket in the back cover. Teachers give feedback on the 2nd drafts in Units 3 and 6. Reflection and goal setting are integral to the learning process and most Units finish with a self-assessment, followed by an invitation to **review** the current Unit, **preview** the website links for the next Unit, **prepare** for the next Unit by looking at the activities in the book, and **organize** the portfolio.

Units 9 and 10 (projects)

The Drama project (Unit 9) allows students to demonstrate how much they have learned in terms of creative speaking and writing, as they devise, design, rehearse, and perform their own mini-dramas. The Print Media project (Unit 10) then encourages them to employ all their newly developed linguistic, social, affective, and cognitive skills in the production of a newspaper, newsletter, magazine, or brochure. The possibilities in both projects are endless. Feedback from students has shown that they really appreciate the opportunity to work together in the design and completion of these projects, and the final results often go beyond the teacher's expectations. Students at all levels and from all majors can be successful in these projects. The role of the teacher at this time is to facilitate learning and to be a learning resource, giving guidance and assistance.

Once the projects are complete, students give performances (Drama project) and presentations (Print Media project), describing the process and product of the project and using the presentation skills acquired in **Freshman English 1**. Both projects are self/peer-assessed as well as teacher-assessed, complementing the formative assessment process that runs throughout the book.

Website

Freshman English 2 has its own Internet website, designed to supplement and reinforce each Unit. The site can be found at: www.finchpark.com/KNUFLE/book-2/. Students and teachers are encouraged to visit this site regularly and to browse the links:

- **Reference sites** (online dictionaries, encyclopedias, thesauruses, etc.);
- **Reading** (reading passages and samples on the theme of the Unit);
- **Writing** (samples and templates for the writing activities);
- **Listening** (online listening activities);
- **Viewing** (related videos);
- **Games & Puzzles** (activities for developing curiosity, creativity, and thinking skills);
- **Links for teachers** (teaching resources relevant to the content of each Unit);
- **Grammar** (study resources and exercises for the Language Workshops);
- **MP3 free downloads** (reading passages and dialogs).

Contents: 1

Units	Engaging (warm-up)	Exploring (speaking)	Reading and Discussing
1 Personally Speaking	Introductions Identity survey	Personal Puzzles Star Signs	Eccentricity Campus Friends: Form-filling
2 Making Plans	Making plans	Top Qualities Occupations Interview	Jobs for the Future Campus Friends: Making plans
3 What's Next?	The next 5, 10, and 20 years	Giving Advice Counseling Role-play	Campus Friends: Preparation
4 That's Life.	Personal Timeline	Important Events Turning Points	Who am I? Campus Friends: Role-play
5 Face to Face	Interviewing Famous People	Interview Role-play Interview Tips	Body Language Campus Friends: Interviewing
6 Work and Play	Making 'To do' and 'Not to do' Lists	Role-play: Traveling Spare Time Survey	Work & Play Campus Friends: Traveling
7 Think Smart	What Sort of Smart?	Career Intelligences Advice Role-play	Multiple Intelligences Campus Friends: Giving Advice
8 That's Entertainment!	Entertainment Preferences	Entertainment Surveys	Entertainment Campus Friends: Sport
9 Drama Project	Theatre Games	Action Stories Role-plays	Campus Friends: Drama
10 Print Media Project	Newspaper Headlines	Looking Back and Looking Ahead	Print media Campus Friends: Reporters
Word Bank	Vocabulary (adjectives) Notional/functional Phrases English-Korean Glossary		

Contents: 2

Explaining (use of language)	Performing (writing)	Reflecting and Reviewing	Pages
Application forms Present (simple, participle)	**Writing an email:** First draft, Peer-editing Final draft	Review of Book 1 Preview (Unit 2) Organization (portfolio)	**1 – 10**
Short bios Present perfect tense	**Writing a short bio:** First draft, Peer-editing Final draft	Book 2 self-assessment Review (Unit 2) Preview (Unit 3) Organization (portfolio)	**11 – 20**
Résumés Brainstorming, outlining	**Résumé:** 1st, 2nd draft, Peer-editing Teacher feedback Final draft	Review (Unit 3) Preview (Unit 4) Organization (portfolio)	**21 – 30**
Autobiographies Simple past tense	**Autobiography:** First draft, Peer-editing Final draft	Reading self-assessment Review (Unit 4) Preview (Unit 5) Organization (portfolio)	**31 – 40**
Follow-up emails Three types of verbs	**Follow-up email:** First draft, Peer-editing Final draft	Speaking self-assessment Review (Unit 5) Preview (Unit 6) Organization (portfolio)	**41 – 50**
Personal statements Coordination & parallelism	**Personal statement:** 1st, 2nd draft, Peer-editing Teacher feedback Final draft	Review (Unit 6) Preview (Unit 7) Organization (portfolio)	**51 – 60**
Cover letters Relative clauses	**Cover letter:** First draft, Peer-editing Final draft	Writing self-assessment Review (Unit 7) Preview (Unit 8) Organization (portfolio)	**61 – 70**
Reviews Active/passive voice	**Review:** First draft, Peer-editing Final draft	Listening Self-assessment Review (Unit 8) Preview (Unit 9) Organization (portfolio)	**71 – 80**
Planning the project Brainstorming, outlining	**Drama project:** First draft, Final draft Rehearsing, Performing	Self/Peer-assessment Review (Unit 9) Preview (Unit 10) Organization (portfolio)	**81 – 96**
Sample newsletter Project checklist	**Print Media project:** Planning Presenting	Self-assessment Group peer-assessment Course feedback	**97 – 112**
Sample bios, résumés, cover letters, personal statements, interview Q & As, follow-up emails		Answer section Assignment flowchart	**113 – 162**

My notes

Unit 1 Personally Speaking

Warm-up Everyone

- Introduce yourself to the person next to you.
- Next, introduce yourself to someone else.
- Try to introduce yourself to everyone in the class.

Campus Friends In this book, we follow six freshman students (2 Koreans and 4 foreign students studying in Korea). Can you match them with their names and nationalities below? Today, they are in the library. What do you think they are talking about?

*This Unit is about filling in forms with personal information and talking about personality.

Identity Survey

Identity includes personal details, preferences (likes, hobbies, wishes), and personality. What do you know about your personal identity? How about your social identity? How about your cultural identity?

Pairs

- Exchange books with the person next to you.
- Ask your partner for the information on this survey (make Wh questions).
- Write his/her answers in the spaces.

IDENTITY SURVEY

Personal details

1. First name ....
2. Last name ....
3. DoB (dd/mm/yy) ....
4. Gender M F ....
5. Hometown ....
6. Blood type ....

Preferences

7. Hobbies ....
8. Favorite color ....
9. Favorite food ....
10. Favorite song ....
    Why? ....
11. Favorite place ....
    Why? ....
12. Favorite proverb ....
    Why? ....
13. Dream job ....
    Why? ....

Personality

14. 3 words that describe you (▶ page 114) ....
15. Something you do well ....
16. Something that is important to you ....
17. Someone who has influenced you ....
18. Your goals in life ....

Groups

- Now introduce your partner to the other people in your group or in the class.

Reading and Discussion: Eccentricity

Track 1

What is your personality? Are you creative, original, and imaginative? These qualities are important, in addition to diligence and responsibility. Here is a magazine article about eccentricity.

Groups • Read the article and then discuss the questions at the bottom of the page.

FE2 Magazine September Issue

Longer life?

Scientists have found that eccentrics are healthier than normal people and live longer. They don't repress their feelings, so they suffer less stress. They are happier and their immune systems work more efficiently. They tend to be optimistic people with a sense of humor, childlike curiosity, and a desire to make the world a better place. They are also highly creative.

Does this sound like you? If it does, then remember that the world needs creative thinkers!

How eccentric are you?

Eccentric people are off-centered. They do things that most people think are odd. However, this does not mean that they are illogical or mentally ill. In fact, eccentric people are often geniuses. They see things in new ways. Their creativity and originality allow them to find brilliant solutions to problems and make great leaps of imagination.

There have been many famous eccentrics. William Spooner (1844-1930) was an Oxford professor who used to misplace letters in a sentence. For example: "Go and shake a tower" ("Go and take a shower"). Oscar Wilde (1854-1900) used to take a lobster for a walk and Sir George Sitwell (1860-1943) had the cows on his estate painted in a blue and white willow pattern. Francis Egerton (1756-1823) was famous for giving dinner parties for dogs and Simeon Ellerton (1702-1799) used to carry stones on his head. Even Sir Isaac Newton (1642-1727) stuck a large needle into his eye, while Albert Einstein (1879-1955) filled his pipe with tobacco from cigarette butts he found in the street.

Discussion questions

1. Are you a creative thinker?
2. Are you an optimist?
   - Why? Why not?
3. Do you want to make the world a better place?
   - How can you do this?
   - Do you have any ideas?
4. Do you know an eccentric person?
   - Describe him/her.
5. Why does the world need eccentrics?

Star Signs

In the West, horoscopes are very popular. Many people think that their star signs affect their personality. In the East, people talk about their animal sign. What do you think? Does astrology control our characters?

By yourself

- Find your star sign on this page. Write your name.
- Ask other people about their star signs. Write their names.
  - When were you born? What star sign are you?

Signs of the Zodiac

♒ Aquarius (water-carrier) (Jan 21 - Feb 19) Name .... Name .... Name .... Name	♓ Pisces (fish) (Feb 20 - March 20) Name .... Name .... Name .... Name	♈ Aries (ram) (March 21 - April 20) Name .... Name .... Name .... Name ....
♉ Taurus (bull) (April 21 - May 21) Name .... Name .... Name .... Name	♊ Gemini (twins) (May 22 - June 21) Name .... Name .... Name .... Name	♋ Cancer (crab) (June 22 - July 22) Name .... Name .... Name .... Name ....
♌ Leo (lion) (July 23 - Aug 22) Name .... Name .... Name .... Name	♍ Virgo (virgin) (Aug 23 - Sept 23) Name .... Name .... Name .... Name	♎ Libra (scales) (Sept 24 - Oct 23) Name .... Name .... Name .... Name ....
♏ Scorpio (scorpion) (Oct 24 - Nov 22) Name .... Name .... Name .... Name	♐ Sagittarius (archer) (Nov 23 - Dec 22) Name .... Name .... Name .... Name	♑ Capricorn (goat) (Dec 23 - Jan 20) Name .... Name .... Name .... Name ....

Groups

- Find the people who have the same birth sign as you.
- Make a group and talk about your birth sign.
- Choose some words that describe all of you (▶ page 114).

People with your star sign are:	....

Campus Friends: Form filling

Track 2

Pairs

- Kadi and Minghua are in the school coffee shop. Read their dialog together.
- You can check the vocabulary in the Glossary (▶ pages 147-154).
- Read the dialog again, changing roles.

Kadi	Hi, Minghua.
Minghua	Good morning, Kadi.
Kadi	What are you looking at?
Minghua	It's an application form for the English newspaper.
Kadi	Are you going to be a reporter? That's a good idea.
Minghua	Yes, but I have to fill in all this personal information.
Kadi	Let's have a look. (Pause) First name, last name, age ...
Minghua	Date of birth, address, school, major, qualifications ...
Kadi	Wow! It's going to take ages to fill it in!
Minghua	Let's get a cup of coffee. We can fill in the form together.
Kadi	Great idea! It's on me today.

Personal Information: Puzzles

Personal information is part of our identity. Here are some puzzles about personal information.

Groups

- Look at puzzles 1 and 2. Can you work out the answers together?
- Look at puzzles 3 to 6. Can you find out this information?

1. Kadi is 19 years old, but she has had only four birthdays. Why do you think this is?

2. Emily is three times as old as she was twelve years ago. How old is she?

3. Deniz is 7,276 days old. How many days have you been alive? How many hours? How many minutes?

4. Do any people in this class share the same birthday?

5. How many people in this class were born on a Monday?

6. What is the average age of people in this class?

*Answers to puzzles 1 and 2 are in the **Answer Section**, at the back of the book.
*You can find the answer to puzzle 3 by searching the Internet for "Age calculator."

Language Workshop: Present Tense

The themes in this book include form filling, bios, and résumés. These all need personal information, including your interests and hobbies. This information is entered using the present tense.

By yourself

- Look at examples 1, and 2. Then write the missing words in 3 and 4.
- Write your own hobbies and pastimes in 5 to 9.

Routine	Hobby
1. I listen to music every day.	My hobby is listening to music.
2. I play soccer every weekend.	My leisure activity is playing soccer.
3. I write in my blog every month.	My pastime is ____________
4. I travel whenever I can.	I am interested in ____________
5. ____________	____________
6. ____________	____________
7. ____________	____________
8. ____________	____________
9. ____________	____________

Pairs

- Fill in this form with the personal information of the Campus Friends.
- The information is on page 1, page 17, and pages 123-125 (short bios).

First name	Last name	Country	Hometown	Hobby
Chang-min	Lee	Korea	Daegu	playing tennis

Notes

* The answers are in the **Answer Section**, at the back of the book.

Application Form: Internship

When you apply for a visa, overseas study, internship, or a job with an international company, you need to fill in forms in English. These ask for personal information, education, qualifications, skills, interests, experience, and objectives (goals).

Pairs

- Exchange books with your partner.
- Fill in this form for your partner by asking suitable questions.

APPLICATION FOR INTERNSHIP

IMS Global Leadership

Personal

Family name ______________________

Given name (s) ______________________

Date of birth (dd/mm/yy) ______________________

Gender ______________________

Nationality ______________________

Passport number ______________________

Remember to attach these documents to this form:

- ☐ Résumé
- ☐ Cover letter
- ☐ Academic transcripts
- ☐ Personal statement
- ☐ Letter of reference
- ☐ Travel insurance

Contact details

Street address ______________________

City ______________________ Country ______________________

Postcode ______________________ Telephone ______________________

Mobile ______________________ Email ______________________

Education

University ______________________

High school ______________________

Prizes and awards ______________________

Clubs and volunteering ______________________

General

Length of stay (weeks) ______________________ Start date (dd/mm/yy) ______________________

Major (1st choice) ______________________ Major (2nd choice) ______________________

English level (speaking) ______________________ English level (writing) ______________________

Other languages ______________________

Objectives ______________________

The information given by me on this form is true and correct, to the best of my belief.

Signature ______________________ Date ______________________

Writing an Email to the Teacher: First Draft

Do you remember writing emails in **Freshman English 1**, Units 1 and 10? Do you remember the 5 parts of an email and the 10 tips for writing emails? You can find them on this page.

By yourself

- Brainstorm what you want to say to the teacher.
- Write the first draft of your email.

1. Subject
2. Greeting
3. Body
4. Closing
5. Signature

1. Meaningful subject
2. Start with a greeting.
3. Identify yourself clearly.
4. Be brief and to the point.
5. Short, simple sentences
6. Formal/informal language
7. No abbreviations/emoticons
8. Re-read, review, and edit.
9. End the email politely.
10. Your name at the end

First draft

To ______________________

Subject ______________________

Attach a file | Receipt On Read : ☐ | Receipt On Delivery : ☐

Cc | Bcc | Signature | Addresses | Save Draft | Send | Check Spelling

____

____

____

____

____

____

____

____

____

____

Pairs

- Exchange books with a classmate for peer-editing.
- Look at the next page for a peer-editing checklist. A marking code is on page 122.

Writing an Email: Second Draft

By yourself

- Revise your first draft based on the feedback from your classmate.
- Send an email of your final draft to your teacher.

To

Subject

Final draft

Attach a file　Receipt On Read :　Receipt On Delivery :

Cc　Bcc　Signature　Addresses　Save Draft　Send　Check Spelling

Pairs

- Here is the checklist for page 8.
- You can also use it to check your final draft.

✓	Peer/Self-Editing Checklist (See page 122)			
☐	Subject	☐	Capital letters	C
☐	Greeting	☐	Punctuation	P
☐	Body	☐	Apostrophes, personal pronouns	Gr1
☐	Closing	☐	Singular/plural, count/non-count	Gr2
☐	Signature	☐	Prepositions	Pr
☐	Paragraph format	☐	Articles	Art

Review: What Can I Do?

Every Unit in this book finishes with a review. This helps you find out what you have learned and what you need to learn. In this Unit we review **Freshman English 1**. Is there anything you need to study again?

By yourself

- Fill in these self-assessment forms and write your scores at the bottom.
- Think about what you can do and what you need to review.

1 = I still don't understand. **2** = I need some help. **3** = I'm OK with this.

Unit	Writing	1	2	3
all	Brainstorming			
all	Mind-mapping			
all	Outlining			
1	Paragraph format			
2	Listing paragraphs			
3	Description paragraphs			
4	Order of importance			
5	Comparison paragraphs			
6	Time order paragraphs			
7	'How to' paragraphs			
8	Process paragraphs			
9	Advantage/disadvantage			
10	Cause and effect			
	My total			

Unit	Grammar	1	2	3
1	Formal/informal			
2	Capital letters			
3	Punctuation			
4	Personal pronouns			
5	Count/non-count			
6	Spelling			
7	Prepositions			
8	Articles			
9	Consistency (S/V)			
10	Word order			
	My total			

Unit	Speaking	1	2	3
all	Conversation			
all	Discussion			
6	Storytelling			
11	Presentations			
	My total			

By yourself

- Review what you have done in this Unit and prepare for the next Unit.

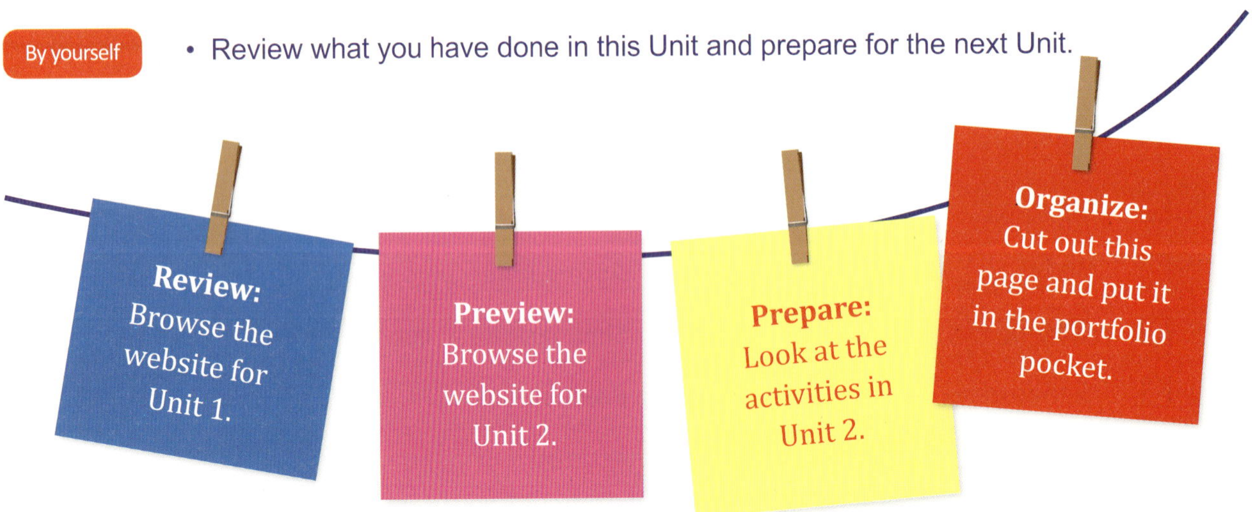

Unit 2 Making Plans

Kadi and Chang-min are making plans. They want to develop themselves in university and they want to prepare for life after they graduate. What do you want to do? What are your plans?

Warm-up Everyone

- Choose activities that you would like to do in university.
- Write them at the bottom of the page.
- Talk about your choices with a classmate.

- Learn how to swim
- Be a volunteer at a festival
- Be a buddy for a visiting exchange student
- Be on the student council
- Do an overseas internship
- Prepare for a career
- Learn a musical instrument
- Volunteer at an international event
- ✓ Learn academic English
- Join the school newspaper
- Learn how to drive
- Do voluntary service
- Join an English conversation club
- Learn another language
- Keep fit
- Be an exchange student
- Make a study group
- Make lots of friends
- Learn how to debate
- Travel

I would like to

*This Unit is about making plans (during and after university) and writing a short bio.

Track 3

Campus Friends: Making Plans

The six friends are talking about their future (▶ page 1). They want to enjoy university life and prepare for their careers. They decide to be reporters on the University English Newspaper.

Groups

- Look at the dialog. Fill in the missing words from the bottom of the page.
- Check the Glossary (▶ pages 147-154) for words that you don't know.
- Read the dialog together a number of times (change roles).

Deniz	Hello everyone. What's new?
Minghua	Hi, Deniz. We're ________ plans.
Deniz	You mean ________ and ________ good grades?
Emily	More than that. We need to develop personally.
Kadi	And we need to prepare for our future.
Chang-min	I'm thinking of __________ for an internship.
Ji-won	I'd like to be an exchange student.
Minghua	If we want good jobs, our résumés must be special.
Deniz	I know what you mean.
Kadi	Employers want to know about student clubs.
Emily	Plus leadership, teamwork, and voluntary service.
Chang-min	I'm __________ of joining a study group.
Ji-won	I'm __________ to work on my academic English.
Kadi	I'm thinking of ________ a reporter on the English newspaper.
Deniz	That's a great idea. You can improve your __________ and __________.
Emily	You're right. Let's all apply to be reporters!

applying	getting	making	studying	writing
being	going	speaking	thinking	

MY NOTES

MY NOTES

*The complete dialog is in the **Answer Section**, at the back of the book.

Top Qualities and Abilities

What do you think are the most important qualities and abilities of good students and job applicants?

Pairs

- Look at the ten qualities and abilities below.
- Put them in your order of importance (1 to 10).
- Talk about them together.
- Here are some words to help you.

as important as	not as important as
more important	less important
more important than	less important than
most important	least important
however	compared with
on the one hand	on the other hand

You		NACE
	Communication skills	
	Computer skills	
	Persuasion skills	
	Analytic skills	
	Writing skills	
	Technical knowledge	
	Planning and organization skills	
	Problem-solving skills	
	Good teamwork skills	
	Information processing skills	

Pairs

- The chart below is based on the *Job Outlook Survey, 2013*, by the National Association of Colleges and Employers (NACE).
- Talk about the chart together.
- Fill in the "NACE" column using the information on the chart.
- Do you agree with NACE?

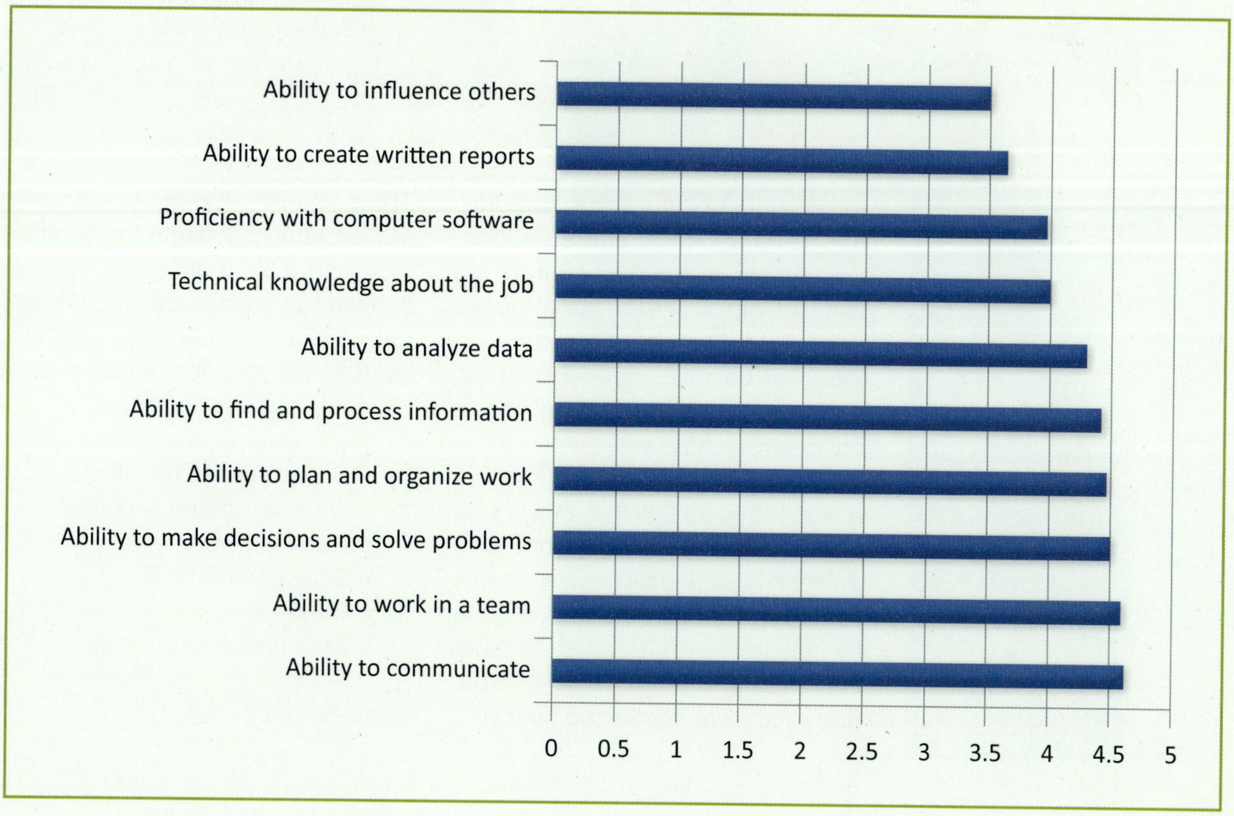

Jobs for the Future

Track 4

Groups

- Read this magazine page together.
- Check the Glossary (▶ pages 147-154) for words that you don't know.
- Talk about your ideas together. Would you like to do any of these jobs?

21st Century Jobs

Fall Issue

What are the top jobs for the 21st century?

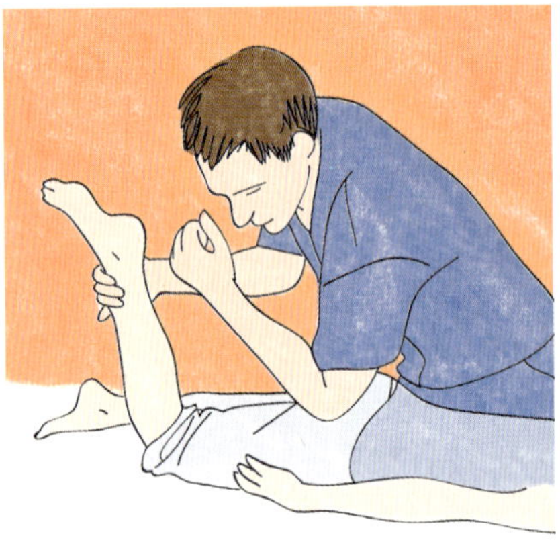

Top jobs

- Software developers
- Physicians and Surgeons
- Software systems developers
- Management analysts
- Computer systems analysts
- Registered nurses
- Civil engineers
- Medical scientists
- Physical therapists
- Dental hygienists
- Biochemical engineers
- Nano-technologists
- Organic farmers
- Robotics technicians
- Waste management consultants

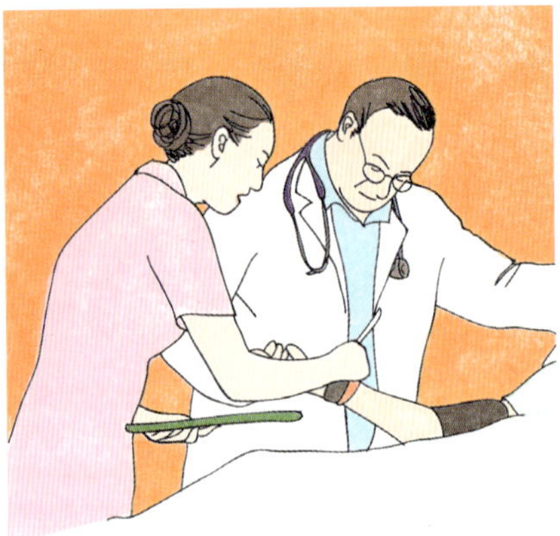

"Your work is going to fill a large part of your life, and the only way to be truly satisfied is to do what you believe is great work. And the only way to do great work is to love what you do. If you haven't found it yet, keep looking. Don't settle. As with all matters of the heart, you'll know when you find it."

Steve Jobs, Stanford, 2005

According to Laurence Shatkin, the author of many career guides, the top jobs in the 21st century will range from software developers to dental hygienists. (See the 'Top jobs' list on this page.) However, many 'hot' jobs of the future have not been invented yet.

If we think about the effects of globalization, automation, and artificial intelligence, then it seems certain that many jobs will be done by machines or outsourced to other countries in the near future. What does this mean for the job seeker?

Thomas Frey, Executive Director of the DaVinci Institute, is Google's top-rated futurist speaker. He says that we will have to be creative and get special education for jobs that cannot be automated or outsourced. Here are some of his ideas:

- Global system architects
- Weather control specialists
- Geoengineers
- Body part makers
- Nano-medics
- Time hackers

What do you think?

* There are more reading passages on the website: www.finchpark.com/KNUFLE/book-2.

Occupations for the 21st Century

As we saw in the reading passage (▶ page 14), jobs are changing very fast these days. Many new jobs are appearing and old jobs are disappearing. Here are some job areas that need more and more people.

Pairs

- Look at the jobs below. Talk about them together.
- Are there any jobs that interest you? Circle them.

Surgeon	Robot technician	Retirement counselor
Pharmacist	Image consultant	Relocation counselor
Biophysicist	Technical writer	Environmental engineer
Veterinarian	Medical assistant	Underwater archaeologist
Job developer	Physical therapist	Network systems analyst
Fitness trainer	Skin care specialist	Computer software engineer
Space mechanic	Home health aide	Special education teacher
Dental assistant	Registered nurse	Leisure sports trainer

Pairs

- Interview a classmate about his/her future job and write the answers on this survey form.

Name ______________________ Date ______________

1. What is your dream job? Why?

2. How can you prepare for your dream job?

3. Which is more important, money or job satisfaction? Why?

4. If you could start a business, what would it be? Why?

5. Do you want a "green job"? Why? Why not?

Language Workshop: Present Perfect

What have you done in your life so far? Think of your education, achievements, relationships, travel, and skills (computers, musical instruments, hobbies, sports, etc.). When we describe these things, we use the present perfect tense: has/have + past participle: I have learned how to swim. I have been to Busan.

By yourself

- Complete the sentences below. Then write your own sentences.

Questions	Answers
1. What have I done?	I have ______________________.
2. Where have I been?	I have been to ______________________.
3. Who has influenced me?	______________________ has influenced me.
4. What ______________________?	______________________.
5. Where ______________________?	______________________.
6. Who ______________________?	______________________.

Groups

- Play the What? Where? Who? game together.
- When you land on a What? Where? or Who? word, talk about what you have done, where you have been, or who you have met.

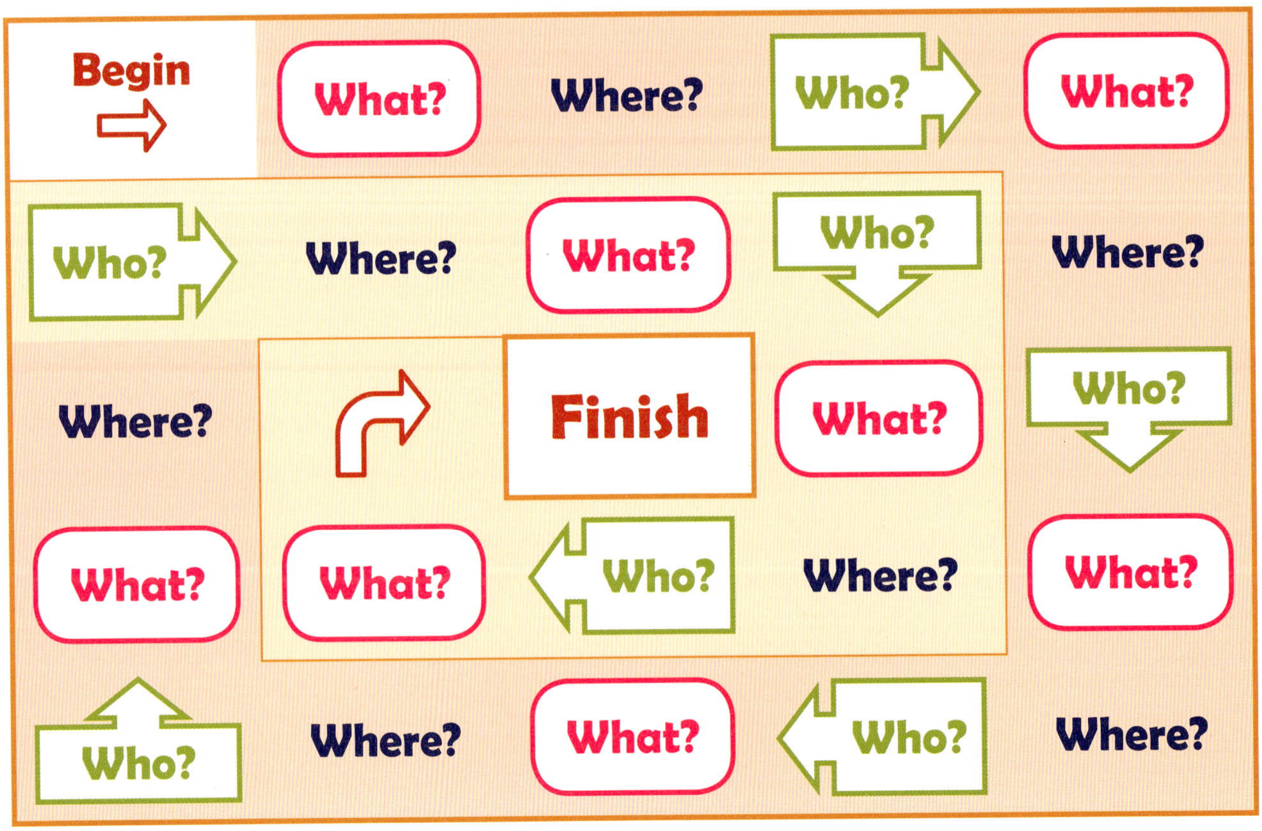

* There are more present perfect activities on the website: www.finchpark.com/KNUFLE/book-2/.

Writing a Short Bio: Sample

Track 5

The Campus Friends want to apply for the school English newspaper (▶ page 12). In order to do this, they have to write their bios. Here is Emily Stounton's bio. There are more sample bios on pages 123 to 125.

By yourself

- Read the bio of Emily Stounton.
- Fill in her information in the notebook, below the bio.

Biodata of Emily Stounton
Drawbridge Lane
Nottingham, UK (Home address)

Emily Stounton became interested in Asian Studies when she was in Walton Grammar School, so she took GCSE 'A' level examinations in Communication and Culture, and Eastern Philosophy. Instead of going to university in the UK, she came to Korea to learn about Korean culture and traditions. Emily worked in a department store during her vacations to earn money to come to Korea. She likes reading and watching documentaries in her spare time and is a member of the university traditional music club. Ms. Stounton wants to be a diplomat and hopes to get an internship with the United Nations. (100 words)

Education:

Jobs:

Interests:

Clubs:

Skills:

Travel:

Prizes:

Future:

* You can see the completed notebook in the **Answer Section**, at the back of the book.

My Short Bio: First Draft

By yourself

- Think about what you have done in your life up to now.
- Fill in your notes below.

Education:

Jobs:

Interests:

Clubs:

Skills:

Travel:

Prizes:

Future:

By yourself

- Now write the first draft of your short bio.
- Look at the samples on pages 17, 123, 124, and 125.

. (words)

My Short Bio: Peer-editing and Final Draft

Pairs

- Exchange your book with a classmate.
- Edit your classmate's first draft (▶ page 18).
- Here is a checklist you can use.

✓	Peer/Self-editing Checklist (▶ page 122)				
☐	Capital letters	C	☐	Punctuation	P
☐	Apostrophes, personal pronouns	Gr1	☐	Singular/plural, count-non-count	Gr2
☐	Spelling	Sp	☐	Articles	Art
☐	Prepositions	Pr	☐	Word order	WO
☐	Subject/Verb/Object agreement	S/v	☐	Present perfect tense (have)	PP
☐	Present tense (routines, hobbies)	PT			

By yourself

- Now write the final draft of your short bio.
- Look at the samples on pages 17, 123, 124, and 125.

____

____

____

____

____

____

____

____

____

____. (words)

Self-assessment: Topics in This Book

What do you know about the topics in this book? Fill in this self-assessment form to find out. You will do this activity again at the end of the book (▶ page 111). At that time you will see how much you have improved.

Pairs

- Exchange books with a classmate.
- Interview him/her about the self-assessment topics in the table below.
  - Do you know how to brainstorm?
- Write 0, 1, 2, or 3 in this column, according to his/her answers.

	Self-assessment Topics	0-3	0-3
1.	Brainstorming, outlining, mind-mapping (every Unit)		
2.	Peer-editing (every Unit)		
3.	Writing an email and filling in forms (Unit 1)		
4.	Writing a bio (Unit 2)		
5.	Applying for a job (Units 3-7)		
6.	Writing a résumé (Unit 3)		
7.	Writing an autobiography (Unit 4)		
8.	Preparing for an interview (Unit 5)		
9.	Writing a personal statement (Unit 6)		
10.	Writing a cover letter (Unit 7)		
11.	Writing a book/film/restaurant review (Unit 8)		
12.	Making and performing a mini-drama (Unit 9)		
13.	Making a newspaper or magazine (Unit 10)		
	Total	**/39**	**/39**

0 = I know nothing about this.
1 = I know a little about this.
2 = I know something, and I want to learn more.
3 = I know everything about this.

Use this column when you self-assess at the end of the course.

By yourself

- Review what you have done in this Unit and prepare for the next Unit.

Review: Browse the website for Unit 2.

Preview: Browse the website for Unit 3.

Prepare: Look at the activities in Unit 3.

Organize: Cut out this page and put it in the portfolio pocket.

Unit 3 What's Next?

In this Unit, you can prepare for the future by learning how to write a résumé in English (writing), and how to give advice (speaking).

Warm-up Everyone

- What will you do in the next 5 years? Draw three pictures.
- How about the next 10 years? Draw three pictures.
- What will you be doing in 20 years' time? Draw three pictures.

Pairs

- Talk about your pictures together.

Giving Advice

When you want to study abroad, apply for a job, or be an intern, it is good to get advice first (▶ page 24). The activity on this page helps you to practice the language of giving advice.

Groups

- Look at the messages that people have posted below and on page 126.
- What advice would you give to these people?
- Use the 'advice' phrases on page 115 and the 'suggesting' phrases on page 121.

I feel very tired these days and I've put on weight. What shall I do?

Chubby

My friend lent me her textbook, but I've lost it. What shall I do?

Forgetful

I want to go to graduate school in the USA, but my TOEFL score is too low. What shall I do?

Desperate

I had an exam today in my major, but I arrived 30 minutes late. What shall I do?

Timeless

I am on the bus to Incheon airport. There is a long traffic jam because of an accident on the expressway. I will miss my plane. What shall I do?

Hopeful

I want to date the person who is dating my best friend. What shall I do?

Confused

My parents scold me all the time. Nothing I do is good enough for them. What shall I do?

Unhappy

My best friend smokes all the time. I hate cigarettes. What shall I do?

Smoked out

My best friend wants to copy my homework. What shall I do?

Concerned

I really want to learn English, but it is too difficult. What shall I do?

Helpless

I try my best in my studies, but I keep getting low grades. What shall I do?

Anxious

I'm very shy and I don't have any friends. No one talks to me. What shall I do?

Lonely

Campus Friends: Preparation

Track 6

In Unit 2, the friends applied to be reporters on the English newspaper. They have been short-listed and have to submit their résumés. They are also thinking of meeting the student counselor (▶ page 24).

Pairs

- Read the dialog together.
- Check the Glossary (▶ pages 147-154) for words that you don't know.
- Read the dialog again (change roles).

Ji-won:	Hello Deniz. Guess what?
Deniz:	You got an e-mail from the editor?
Ji-won:	That's right! How did you know?
Deniz:	I think we all got one. We're all short-listed.
Ji-won:	You mean we have to submit a résumé?
Deniz:	Yes! This is great practice for later, when we apply for jobs.
Ji-won:	What sort of job do you want?
Deniz:	I'm thinking of being a geotechnical engineer.
Ji-won:	Wow! That sounds amazing. I'd like to be a food consultant.
Deniz:	There are lots of new jobs these days.
Ji-won:	I know. I really need to talk to someone about my career.
Deniz:	Why don't you go to the student job counselor?
Ji-won:	I didn't know there was one.
Deniz:	Of course. She's in the Student Affairs building.
Ji-won:	Great! I'll send her an e-mail and make an appointment.
Deniz:	Why don't we go together? I have some questions as well.

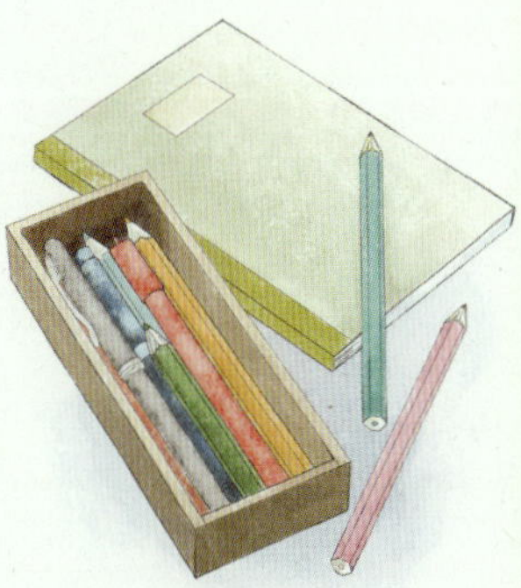

My notes

Role-play: Student Counseling

You have made an appointment to see the student counselor for career advice. What will you say to the counselor? What advice will he/she give you?

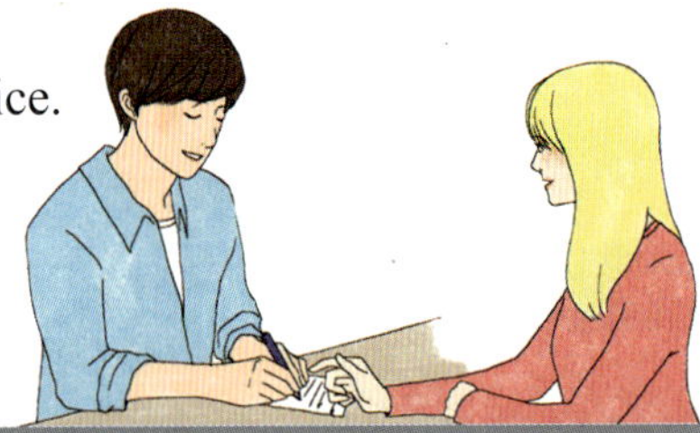

By yourself

- Fill in the "Student Information Form" below.

Student Information Form

Name ______________ Student ID ______________

1. Why are you visiting the counselor? ______________
2. What are your life goals? ______________
3. How can you achieve your goals? ______________
4. Who is your role model? ______________
5. What is your dream job? ______________
6. Have you thought of any other jobs? ______________
7. Do you want to work abroad? ______________

Pairs

- Exchange books. Choose roles (**Student A** or **Student B**).
- **Student A**: You are the counselor.
  - Ask student B about the answers on his/her Student Information Form.
  - Give advice to student B. Use the 'advice' phrases on page 115 and the 'suggesting' phrases on page 121.
- **Student B**: You are the student.
  - Ask the counselor (Student A) the questions below.
  - Use the conversation phrases on page 116.

Counselor Question Form

1. What job do you recommend? ______________
2. How can I prepare for that job? ______________
3. What qualifications do I need? ______________
4. Do I need to take an English exam? ______________
5. What would you do if you were me? ______________

Pairs

- Change roles and do the role-play again.

Sample Résumé

Here is a one-page résumé. There are more sample résumés in the Word Bank (▶ pages 127-129) and on the website for this Unit: www.finchpark.com/KNUFLE/book-2/unit03/.

Groups

- Look at the sample résumé together.
- Talk about the notes in the sidebar.

Not all résumés need a photo or gender. Check the application information.

Ji-won Moon

Personal Information

Address: Moojigae APT 101-910, Hwarang-dong 123, Nam-gu
Gyeongju, Gyeongsangbuk-do 780-954
Republic of Korea
Tel: +82 (0)54-789-0123; Cell: +82 (0)17-987-6543
E-mail: JMoon@kmail.net
Date of Birth: May 16, 1993
Gender: Female
Nationality: Korean

Objective

A career in the food industry as a nutritionist or food consultant

Education

Kyungpook National University, Korea — 2012 - present
Bachelor of Science (Expected February 2016)

Major: Nutrition and Food Science

Gyeongju High School — 2009 - 2012

Work Experience

Teaching Korean to foreigners — 2012 - present

Honors and Activities

President, English Conversation Club (Gyeongju High School)
English Summer School Diploma (Hati College, Indonesia)
Volunteering in an orphanage (Gyeongju City)

Skills

Computer: MS Office, Hangul, Photoshop
English: TOEIC score 690
Cooking: KNCI Certificate (Advanced)
Driving License

Interests

Cooking, swimming, playing guitar, reading, sketching

References

Available on request

- Highlight the headings or write them in capital letters.
- Country code (Korea = 82)
- Local code. In international calls, '054' becomes '54.'
- Simple e-mail address
- Career goals
- Education in reverse time order
- Full and part-time jobs
- Prizes, clubs, activities, summer school, etc.
- Computer, languages, certificates
- Balance of interests (mind and body)
- Look at the tips on page 26 and the résumés on pages 127-129.

Tips for Making a Résumé

Here are some résumé tips. Look at these when you make your drafts (▶ pages 28-30).

Pairs • Look at the tips and talk about them together.

Personal Information

- Put your personal information and contact information at the top.

Objective

- Show that you have a plan, a direction, and a goal.

Education

- Include university, college (▶ page 130), high school, and other schools or programs.

Work Experience

- Include work experience, plus part-time work.
- Add a bulleted list of responsibilities for each job (▶ page 128).
    - o Don't worry. You still have time to add qualifications and activities to your résumé.
    - o How about joining some clubs and taking extra courses (computer skills, writing, etc.)?

Honors and Awards

- Write down any special achievements or prizes.
    - o They show that you can work hard and achieve your goals.

Skills

- Show that you have computer skills, foreign language skills, and creative skills.
- Don't add unnecessary information and don't use 'buzz' words (e.g. 'dynamic', 'innovative').

Activities and Interests

- Write about clubs and activities. Were you ever a president? Student representative?
    - o These show that you are a team player and that you have leadership skills.

References

- Check the application details to see if you need to give any referees. (▶ pages 128, 129).
- If not, you can write 'References available on request' (▶ pages 25, 127).

Finally ...

- Keep your résumé to one page and use a simple, easy-to-read font.
- Use high quality white paper and make the résumé look attractive and tidy.
- Do a spell-check, a grammar-check, and a punctuation-check.
- Don't use the same résumé every time. Change it to suit the job.

Résumé Dos and Don'ts

This crossword helps us remember what to do (dos) and what not to do (don'ts) when making a résumé. The answers to the clues are on pages 25 and 26. They are also at the bottom of this page, but the letters have been mixed up.

Groups

- Look at the crossword clues together. Talk about them.
- Fill in the missing letters in the crossword.

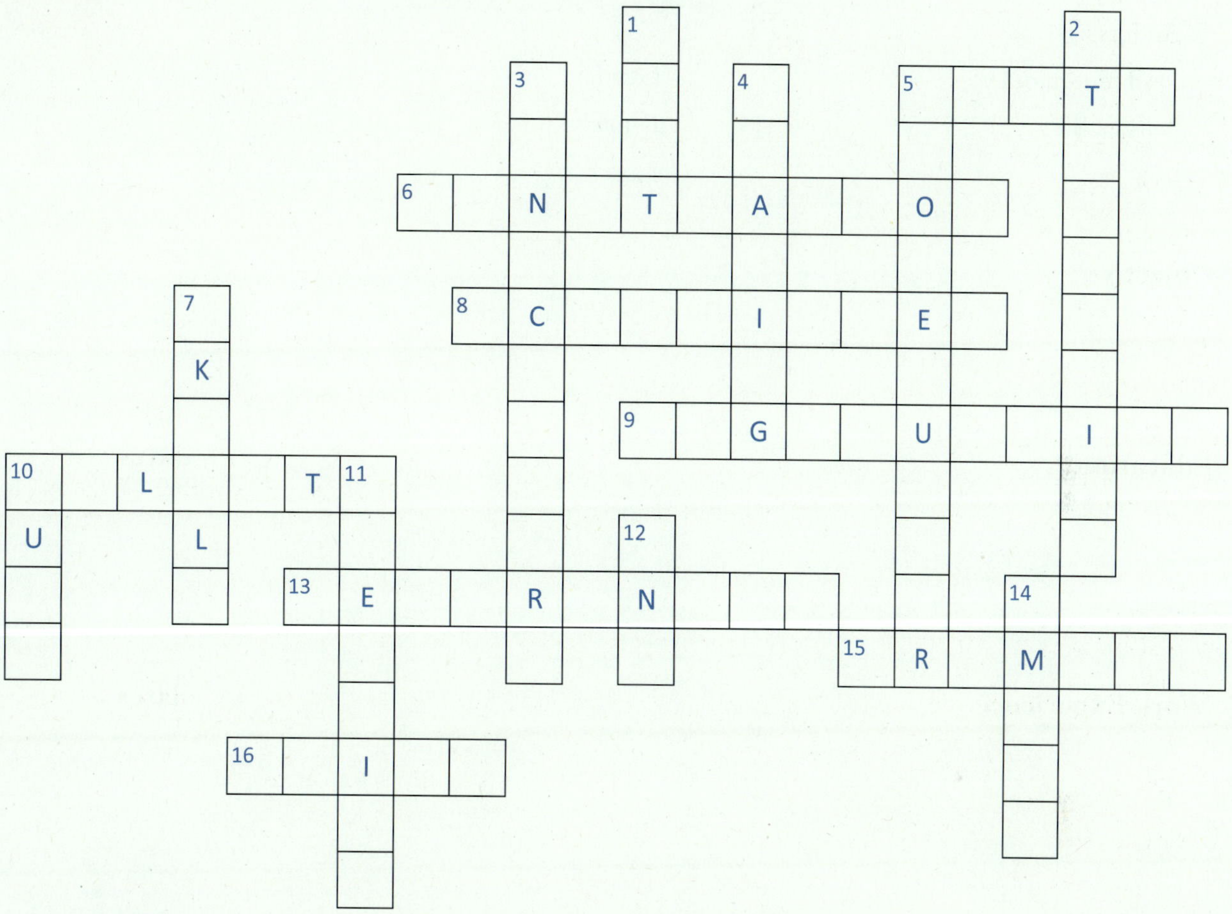

Clues Across

5 Not all résumés have a .... at the top.
6 This is one of the three checks you should do before you finish.
8 Write about clubs and ....
9 Use .... paper.
10 Use these to list responsibilities.
13 Check the application details to see if you need to give these.
15 One of the 3 checks you should do.
16 Use .... paper, not colored paper.

Clues Down

1 This should be simple and easy to read.
2 Make the résumé look .... and tidy.
3 Don't add .... information.
4 Highlight each .... or use capital letters.
5 Add the country code with your ....
7 Include your computer .... and language ....
10 Don't use .... words like 'innovative'.
11 One of the three checks you should do.
12 Keep your résumé to this number of pages.
14 Use a simple .... address.

LPLGEISN GMMARRA PAUITUNNOCT OPOTH ITEWH ENO GEHADIN NFTO EBTULLS RAENSUSYECN NEFCSREEER BZZU EITITSAIVC KSISLL IAMEL UEEOBNPHNMR IAGLYHHIQUT VRIAATETTC

*The completed crossword is in the **Answer Section**, at the back of the book.

My Résumé: First Draft

By yourself

- Fill in your details on this résumé template.
- Look at page 130 to find the name of your department in English.

Personal Information

Address:

DoB (dd/mm/yy): Gender:

Nationality: E-mail:

Tel: Fax:

Objective

Education

dates (mm/yy)

-
-
-

Work Experience

dates (mm/yy)

-
-
-

Honors and Awards

dates (mm/yy)

-
-

Skills

Activities and Interests

Pairs

- Exchange books with a classmate for peer-editing.
- Check your classmate's résumé for spelling and clarity (▶ pages 25, 26, 27).

My Résumé: Second Draft

By yourself

- Choose a format (▶ pages 25, 127-129) and rewrite your résumé.
- If you are making a digital résumé, look for MS Office templates online, check the KNUFLE website, or search for "Europass CV Generator".

By yourself

- Cut out this page and give your résumé to your teacher for feedback and comments.

My Résumé: Final Draft

By yourself

- Look at the feedback from your teacher.
- Rewrite your résumé by hand or using a computer.
- Put the final draft in the portfolio pocket.

Follow-up

- Review what you have done in this Unit and prepare for the next Unit.

Review: Browse the website for Unit 3.

Preview: Browse the website for Unit 4.

Prepare: Look at the activities in Unit 4.

Organize: Put your final draft in the portfolio pocket.

Unit 4 That's Life.

What are the main events in your life so far? Are there any that you will always remember?
You can learn how to write your autobiography in English in this Unit.

Warm-up Everyone

- Write eight main events of your life on the timeline below.
  - When were you born (date, time, place)?
  - When and where did you go to school? Did anything special happen?
  - Have you ever moved home? Have you ever traveled?

Years	
0-2	
3-5	
6-8	
9-11	
12-14	
15-17	
18-20	
21-23	

Pairs

- Talk about your timelines together.

Brainstorming: Important Events

By yourself

- Choose four of the main events on page 31 and give each event a title.
- Write one title in each jigsaw piece on this page.
- Write four key words about each event (what, where, when, why, etc.).

1: ______________

1. ______________
2. ______________
3. ______________
4. ______________

2: ______________

1. ______________
2. ______________
3. ______________
4. ______________

3: ______________

1. ______________
2. ______________
3. ______________
4. ______________

4: ______________

1. ______________
2. ______________
3. ______________
4. ______________

Campus Friends: Role-play

Track 7

Chang-min and Emily are preparing for their interviews. They are looking at Question 1, on page 44: "Tell me something about yourself."

Pairs

- Read the dialog together.
- Check the Glossary (▶pages 147-154) for words that you don't know.

Emily: OK, Chang-min, shall we start? You can be the interviewer.

Chang-min: Right. Good morning, Ms. Stounton. Tell me about yourself.

Emily: I'm interested in Asian Studies and I want to be a diplomat.

Chang-min: I see. Tell me about the main events in your life.

Emily: Well, I worked in a department store.

Chang-min: And why was this event special?

Emily: It taught me the value of serving people.

Chang-min: Any other events?

Emily: Yes. I played in a traditional music concert.

Chang-min: That sounds interesting.

Emily: It was. It taught me about diligence and teamwork.

Chang-min: Thank you. Let's move on to another question ...

Pairs

- Make your own role-play, based on your most important events (▶page 32).
- **[Interviewer]** Ask why the events were special.

My role-play notes

Reading: Who am I?

Track 8

Groups

Here is a magazine arts page. It has the autobiography of a famous Renaissance man. Can you guess who it is? Read the articles and do the activity at the bottom.

Arts Page

Do you know who I am?

I was born near Florence, Italy, on April 15, 1452, at 10:30 pm. Many people think that I was one of the greatest painters in history, though only 15 of my paintings remain. Two of these, *The Last Supper* and the *Mona Lisa*, can be seen everywhere, on T-shirts, posters, and textbooks.

The term 'Renaissance man' describes people who do lots of things very well. I was the original Renaissance man, since I was a sculptor, architect, musician, engineer, inventor, anatomist, geologist, mapmaker, botanist, and writer. I designed an airplane, a helicopter, a tank, and a calculator, long before the technology existed to make them. I even thought of using the sun for energy.

I started my own workshop in Florence when I was 20 and produced my first drawing in 1473. In 1483, I went to Milan, where I painted *The Last Supper* (1498), but I left in 1499, because of the war between Italy and France.

More about me

I returned to Florence, where my father died in 1504. Then I went back to Milan in 1506, Florence in 1507, and Milan again in 1508. During this time (1504-08) I painted the *Mona Lisa*. In 1513, I worked at the Vatican in Rome. In 1516, King Francis 1 of France asked me to make a mechanical lion and gave me a house in Amboise, where I died in 1519.

Because I was left-handed, I wrote in my notebooks from right to left, as if in a mirror. I have been called the most famous left-handed artist ever.

Write the important events of this person's life on the timeline below.

1452 born							1519 died
1450	1460	1470	1480	1490	1500	1510	1520

*The name of this person is in the **Answer Section**, at the back of the book.

*More autobiographies can be found on the website: www.finchpark.com/KNUFLE/book-2/.

Who am I?: Discussion

Pairs

- Discuss these questions about the reading passages (▶page 34).
- Write your group's answers below the questions.

1. Would you like to be a Renaissance man/woman?

2. What are you good at? What can you do well?

3. Are left-handed people more talented than right-handed people?

4. What would the person on page 34 do if he were alive today?

5. Do you know a multi-talented person? Tell us about him/her.

Pairs

- These famous people changed their names or made stage names.
- Can you find their original names? What do you know about these people?

Changed name or stage name	Original name
Mother Teresa	Agnes Gonxha Bojaxhiu
Mark Twain	Charles Lutwidge Dodgson
Lewis Carroll	Eric Arthur Blair
George Orwell	Jung Ji-hoon
Lenin	Kwon Bo-a
Bill Clinton	Norma Jeane Mortenson
Marilyn Monroe	Reginald Kenneth Dwight
Elton John	Samuel Langhorne Clemens
Rain	Vladimir Ilyich Ulyanov
BoA	William Jefferson Blythe III

*The answers are in the **Answer Section**, at the back of the book.

Sample Autobiography

Track 9

Here is Deniz's autobiography. It is based on his bio (page 125).

Groups

- Read the autobiography together. What key events has Deniz written about?
- How did the events make him feel? Did the events change his life?

My Autobiography: Deniz Osman

There have been a number of important events in my life. The first thing I remember is when I was 5 years old, and my family visited the zoo. I loved seeing all the animals. I think this led to my love of nature. Soon after this, I started elementary school. My 6th grade teacher used to say, "If a thing's worth doing, it's worth doing well." I never understood what she meant until I became a volunteer at engineering fairs in Ankara. It was difficult for me at first, but the company representatives told me, "Happiness comes from hard work." It was like a light turning on in my brain. From that point, I have never given up on anything. When I start something, I always finish it. The proverb really is true, "Well begun is half done."

Another important event happened when I was on the school soccer team. A player on the other team fouled me, but the referee penalized me instead. Because of this, the other player had a free kick and scored a goal. We lost the game. I was very upset, and I was angry with the referee. However, the coach told me, "It's no use crying over spilt milk." He said it was more important to take part than to win.

Sometimes we have good luck and sometimes we have bad luck. The important thing is to do our best. I have never forgotten the coach's words and they have helped me whenever I have had troubles. I am grateful for all the lessons I have had and I hope to live a life helping others.

Language Workshop: Simple Past Tense

When we write our autobiography (▶ page 36) or talk about our achievements (▶ page 33) we use the past tense. The endings of regular verbs are pronounced three different ways: /d/ (laughed), /t/ (asked), and /id/ (needed). Irregular verbs have different rules: sit/sat, hit/hit.

Pairs • Look at the regular verbs below. Write them in the correct columns (/d/, /t/, or /id/).

arrived	cleaned	ended	lasted	lived	~~rested~~	stayed	wanted	watched
~~asked~~	cried	landed	~~saved~~	needed	stopped	walked	washed	worked

/d/	/t/	/id/	Irregular
1 saved	1 asked	1 rested	1
2	2	2	2
3	3	3	3
4	4	4	4
5	5	5	5
6	6	6	6
			7
			8

*The completed table is in the **Answer Section**, at the back of the book.

Pairs • Look at Deniz's autobiography (▶page 36), and do the following tasks together.

1. Find the verbs that are in the past tense.
2. Write them in the table (/d/, /t/, /id/, or irregular).
3. Find Deniz's important events. How many are there?
4. Underline the topic and conclusion sentences.
5. Find two proverbs. What do they mean?

*Proverbs are very useful for autobigraphies and personal statements. You can find more proverbs on page 146.

Autobiography: First Draft

Why were your important events (▶ page 32) special? Did they make you very happy or very sad? Did they help you make a decision? Were they turning points? Did they change your life?

By yourself

- Look at the autobiography tips (below) and Deniz's autobiography (▶ page 36).

Tips for writing an autobiography

1. Think about your key events. What did you learn from them?
2. What ideas and values are important to you? Who is your role model?
3. Make the reader interested. For example, use a proverb (▶ page 146) or a surprising idea.
4. Use "I". The autobiography is about you, your feelings, and your important ideas.
5. Don't try to write about everything that has happened to you.

- Write your first draft, using the events on page 32.
- Ckeck out the adjectives on page 114.

TITLE

TOPIC SENTENCE

1

2

3

4

CONCLUSION

Pairs

- Show your first draft to a classmate. Ask him/her to edit it.

My Autobiography: Final Draft

By yourself

- Rewrite your autobiography, based on your classmate's feedback.
- Make it interesting and meaningful. You can add pictures.
- You can type your autobiography and stick it here if you wish.

Self-assessment: My Reading Skills

What level are your reading skills? How can you improve your reading? This self-assessment is based on the European Council's DIALANG. You can learn more about DIALANG on the website for this Unit.

By yourself

- Read the sentences below.
- Check (✓) the statements that apply to you.
- What is your reading level?

LEVEL	Self-assessment statements: Reading	✓
A1	I can understand simple texts, especially if they contain pictures.	
A1	I can understand short texts, with familiar words and basic phrases.	
A1	I can follow short, simple written instructions.	
A1	I can recognise words and simple phrases on notices.	
A2	I can understand simple texts related to my major.	
A2	I can find information in advertisements, menus, and timetables.	
A2	I can understand simple e-mails.	
A2	I can understand signs and notices in public places.	
B1	I can search texts to find information for completing a task.	
B1	I can recognise the main points in newspaper articles.	
B1	I can identify the conclusions in simple texts.	
B1	I can understand instructions on electrical equipment.	
B2	I can read many types of texts quite easily.	
B2	I understand most of the words when I read a text.	
B2	I can identify the main points in news items, articles, and reports.	
B2	I can understand articles and reports about current affairs and problems.	

By yourself

- Review what you have done in this Unit and prepare for the next Unit.

Review: Browse the website for Unit 4.

Preview: Browse the website for Unit 5.

Prepare: Look at the activities in Unit 5.

Organize: Put this page in the portfolio pocket.

Unit 5 Face to Face

You have won a trip in a time machine. You can travel back into history and interview anyone you want to. However, you only have three questions. Who will you interview?

Warm-up Everyone

- Write the name of the person you want to interview.
- Write the three questions that you want to ask.

I want to interview: --

My first question: --

My second question: --

My third question: --

Cleopatra, Jesus Christ, Steve Jobs, Carl Jung, Shin Saimdang, Mohammad, Christopher Columbus, Marilyn Monroe, Abraham Lincoln, Mahatma Gandhi, Leonardo da Vinci, Kim Yu-shin, John Lennon, Yu Gwan-sun, Walt Disney, Vincent van Gogh, Michelangelo, Yi Sun-shin, Mark Twain, Alexander Graham Bell, Ludwig van Beethoven, Leo Tolstoy, Diana Spencer, Napoleon, Julius Caesar, Pablo Picasso, Martin Luther King, Elvis Presley, Lee Hwang, King Sejong, Isaac Newton, Charles Dickens, Wolfgang Amadeus Mozart, Mother Teresa, John F. Kennedy, Albert Einstein, George Washington, Jane Austen, Vincent van Gogh, Charles Darwin, William Shakespeare

Pairs

- Talk about your choices and your questions together.
- Role-play your interview with the historical person.

*This Unit looks at interview skills (speaking) and 'thank you' emails (writing).

Campus Friends: Interviewing

Track 10

Kadi and Minghua are also preparing for their interviews (see Unit 4, ▶page 33). They are playing the "Why?" interview game. Kadi's interview tips are on page 44.

By yourself

- Read the dialog together.
- Check the Glossary (▶pages 147-154) for any words you don't know.
- Read the dialog again. Change roles.

Minghua:	Hello, Kadi. Do you have a moment?
Kadi:	Of course, Minghua. What is it?
Minghua:	Do you have any tips for the newspaper interview?
Kadi:	Sure. I have lots of sample questions and answers.
Minghua:	Can you send them to me?
Kadi:	OK. Do you want to play an interview game?
Minghua:	That sounds like a good idea. How do we play it?
Kadi:	Just answer my questions as quickly as you can.
Minghua:	Right. Let's begin.
Kadi:	Why do you want to be a reporter?
Minghua:	I want to write about school life.
Kadi:	Why?
Minghua:	Um ... I like finding things out.
Kadi:	Why?
Minghua:	Er ... It's interesting.
Kadi:	Why?
Minghua:	This is difficult. I think it's my turn to ask you.

Pairs

- Play the "Why?" interview game together.
- Make your own topic.

My notes

*There are more interview resources on the website: www.finchpark.com/KNUFLE/book-2/unit05/.

Reading: Body Language

Track 11

Groups Here is a magazine page about body language. Read the article together and discuss the Dos and Don'ts. You can check the vocabulary in the Word Bank.

Special Issue

COMMUNICATION WEEKLY

Body Language

When we have an interview for a job, graduate school, or an internship, body language is very important. It tells the interviewer what sort of person we are. Interviewers look at body language to find information about us that is not in the résumé.

Experts say that 70% of our communication is through non-verbal language such as body language. This includes our posture (how we sit or stand), the way we use our hands, the gestures we make, our facial expressions, our eye movements, our body movements, proxemics (the distance between us and the other person), and even our breathing.

When you are preparing for an interview, be sure to check your body language. Stand in front of a mirror (or make a video of yourself) and practice answering sample interview questions. Use this checklist:

- ☐ How is my posture?
- ☐ What are my hands doing?
- ☐ How about my arms?
- ☐ How about my legs?
- ☐ Am I making eye contact?
- ☐ Am I smiling?
- ☐ How is my facial expression?
- ☐ Do I look confident?
- ☐ Does my body language say that I am the best person for the position?

CONTENTS

Gestures: What do they mean? How do they differ from country to country?

Eye contact: Is it always a good idea to look someone in the eye?

Facial expressions: Do you know what your face is saying to other people?

Proxemics: How close is 'too close'? The new science of personal space.

Personality test: What does your body language tell you about yourself?

The human body is the best picture of the human soul. - Ludwig Wittgenstein

Interview Body Language: Dos and Don'ts

Do:

1. Wear clean, smart, professional clothes.
2. Smile, even on phone interviews.
3. Make eye contact and look interested.
4. Sit up straight, both feet on the floor.
5. Nod your head and be positive.
6. Look at all the interviewers.
7. Keep a good space between you and the interviewers.
8. Look confident and professional all the time you are in the interview building.

Don't:

1. Wear casual clothes and trainers.
2. Look worried, anxious, or bored.
3. Fold your arms across your chest.
4. Cross and uncross your legs.
5. Rub your head, neck, or nose.
6. Look away from the interviewers.
7. Move your hands or make too many gestures.
8. Lean back in your seat.
9. Answer your cell phone.
10. Wear lots of perfume or after-shave.

*There are more reading passages on the website: www.finchpark.com/KNUFLE/book-2/unit05/read.html.

Ask the Experts: Interview Tips

Do you know how to prepare for an interview? Kadi asked online for some interview tips. These are the ones she gave to Minghua on page 42.

Groups • Read the web page together and discuss the interview tips.

ASK THE EXPERTS and get a great job

Home | Resources | Sample interviews | Q &A | Contact us

Date: 16.10.2014 | Posted by Kadi

Dear interview experts,
I am an international student studying in Korea. I have an English interview next week for the school newspaper. Can you give me some interview tips?

Read more » 11 comments

Interview tips for Kadi

Date: 17.10.2014 | Posted by Interview Pro

Hello Kadi,
Welcome to 'Ask the Experts' and thank you for your question. Here are some tips for you. I hope they are useful. Good luck!

Read more » 7 comments

Check these out:

Cover letters
Résumé templates
Personal statements
Follow-up e-mails
Archives

Calendar

October

Su	Mo	Tu	We	Th	Fr	Sa
			1	2	3	4
5	6	7	8	9	10	11
12	13	14	15	16	17	18
19	20	21	22	23	24	25
26	27	28	29	30	31	

« September November »

Before the interview

Check out the website of the school/company.
Practice interview Q&As with a friend.
Check your body language.
Read your résumé and personal statement.
Wear smart clothes.
Set out early and take copies of your résumé.
Take a pen and paper.

During the interview

Smile and be polite.
Use positive body language.
Use formal language.
Answer calmly and honestly.
Answer fully. Don't just say "Yes" or "No."
Ask questions about the company.
Show that you have researched the company.

When you get there

Arrive 10-15 minutes early.
Greet the assistant politely.
Ask what you should do.
Find the interview room.
Turn off your cell phone.
Sit down. Prepare quietly.
Breathe deeply. Think positively.

At the end of the interview

Thank the interviewers.
Ask if you can send a follow-up e-mail.

Interview Role-Play

You learned about body language on page 43. Now it's time to think about what you will say in the interview. Here are 20 common interview questions. You can see sample answers on pages 131-133.

Pairs

- Make an interview role-play (applicant, interviewer).
  - **Applicant:** Decide what you are aplying for: job, scholarship, internship, etc.
  - **Interviewer:** Choose some questions and interview the applicant.
  - **Applicant:** Answer clearly and confidently (▸pages 131-133).
- When you have finished, change roles.

Interview questions

1. Tell me something about yourself.
2. How would you describe yourself?
3. Tell me about your education.
4. How did you choose your college/university?
5. How do you prepare for tests or exams?
6. Who was your best teacher? Why?
7. What is your greatest strength?
8. What is your greatest weakness?
9. Describe your work or study style.
10. How do you manage stress and pressure?
11. Are you a motivated person?
12. What are you passionate about?
13. What makes you angry?
14. Are you a team player?
15. What have you learned from your mistakes?
16. How has university life prepared you for a career?
17. Why did you apply for this job/position/internship/scholarship?
18. Why are you the best person for this job/position/internship?
19. What do you know about this job/company/school?
20. What are your goals for the next 5/10/15 years?

*There are more interview resources on the website: www.finchpark.com/KNUFLE/book-2/.

Language Workshop: Three Types of Verbs

When we have an interview, we need to speak clearly and correctly. In addition, there are three types of verbs we need to know about. You can see examples of these verbs in the Word Bank (▶ page 134).

Type 1: verb + to + infinitive complement

- I hope to graduate soon.
- She decided to join a conversation club.

Example verbs:

ask	choose	expect	know	mean	offer	promise	want
care	decide	hope	learn	need	plan	wait	wish

Pairs

- Make your own Type 1 sentences together.
- Share your sentences with another pair of classmates.

1

Type 2: verb + gerundive complement

- I enjoy swimming.
- He finished writing his assignment.

Example verbs:

go	keep	enjoy	admit	dislike	discuss	imagine	consider
risk	miss	finish	advise	escape	suggest	practice	understand

Pairs

- Make your own Type 2 sentences together.
- Share your sentences with another pair of classmates.

2

Type 3: verb + infinitive or gerund

- She began training for the marathon.
- She began to train.

Example verbs:

see	like	hate	stop	cease	prefer	continue
try	love	start	begin	forget	regret	remember

Pairs

- Make your own Type 3 sentences together.
- Share your sentences with another pair of classmates.

3

After the Interview: Follow-up Email

Track 12

It is a good idea to send a 'thank you' email after the interview. Here are two sample emails. Deniz is following up the newspaper interview, and Emily is following up her interview for a summer camp.

Groups
- Look at the emails together.
- Discuss the format, the language (formal/informal), and the content.

To "Professor Lee" <leeshinmun@abc.ac.kr>
Subject Thank you for the interview: D. Osman
Attach a file Receipt On Read : ☐ Receipt On Delivery : ☐
Cc Bcc Signa… …aft Send Che…

Polite thanks

Deniz is still interested and mentions his strong points.

Dear Professor Lee,

Thank you for giving me an interview for the school English newspaper. It was good to have the chance to talk with you, and I could see your passion for helping students.

I am very interested in becoming a reporter, for my own development, and to contribute to the school. As an international student, I feel that I can offer a new perspective.

Thank you again. I look forward to hearing from you.

Politely asking for news about the interview.

Yours sincerely,

Deniz Osman
017-123-4567

Contact information

Polite thanks for the interview, with positive comments about the camp.

To "Director Kim" <kimho@summercamp.or.kr>
Subject Thanks from Emily Stounton
Attach a file Receipt On Read : ☐ Receipt On Delivery : ☐
Cc Bcc Signature Addresses Save Draft Send Che…

Emily is still very interested and mentions her strong points.

Dear Ms. Kim, Han-ok,

Thank you for interviewing me yesterday about the summer camp. It was a good chance to learn about the camp and talk with you about it. I could see that the summer camp is very well organized. I hope I will become a member of the teaching team.

Coming from the UK, I feel that I have a lot to offer the children on the camp. I can tell them about British culture as well as making the English language enjoyable for them.

Thank you for giving me your time. I hope to hear from you soon.

Sincerely yours,

Politely asking for news about the interview.

Emily Stounton
018-987-6543

Contact information

Follow-up Email: First Draft

You made an interview role-play on page 45. Now you are going to write a follow-up email.

By yourself

- First, decide what position you applied for: full-time job, scholarship, internship, etc.
- Next, brainstorm what you want to say and write your first draft.

Brainstorming (Look at page 47.)

Pairs

- Exchange your first draft with a classmate for peer-editing.

*Check out the sample follow-up emails on the website: www.finchpark.com/KNUFLE/book-2/unit05/.

Follow-up Email: Final Draft

By yourself

- Rewrite your follow-up email based on the feedback from your classmate.
- You can write it or you can type it and stick it on this page.
- You can send a real email to your teacher if he/she agrees.

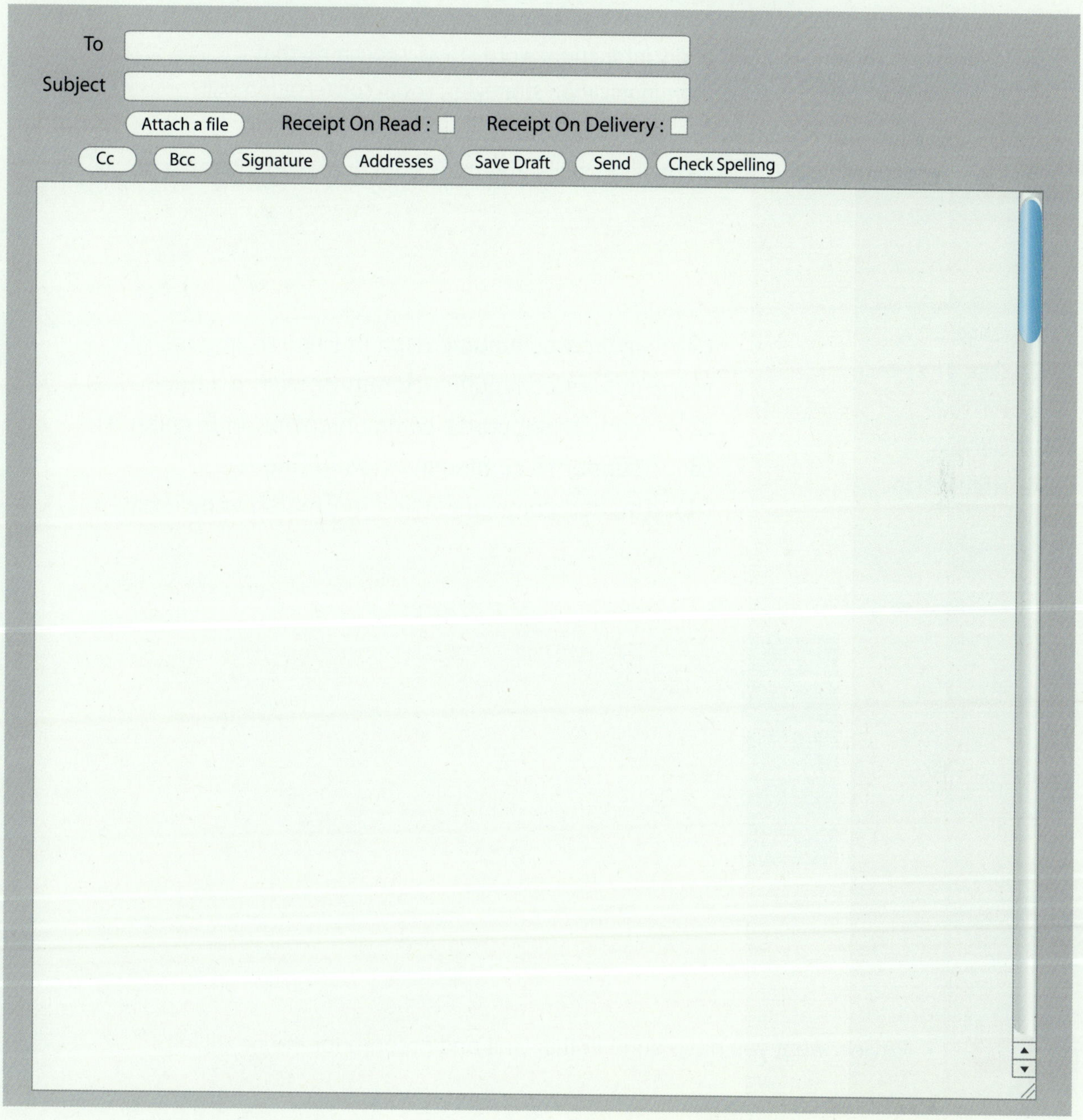

Self-assessment: My Speaking Skills

What level are your speaking skills? How can you improve them? This self-assessment looks at five aspects of speaking.

1. **Range**: vocabulary, grammar
2. **Ease of speech**: fluency, lack of hesitation, speed
3. **Attitude**: confidence, motivation, positive attitude
4. **Delivery**: volume, pronunciation, intonation, word-stress, speech-rhythm
5. **Interaction**: body language, communication strategies, social conversation skills

By yourself

- Assess your English speaking skills and mark your scores in the table below.

My range ...
My ease of speech...
My attitude ...
My delivery ...
My interaction ...

(0) ··· makes communication in English impossible.
(1) ··· makes communication in English difficult.
(2) ··· almost supports communication in English.
(3) ··· supports communication in English.
(4) ··· makes communication in English very easy.

4					
3					
2					
1					
0					
	R	E	A	D	I

By yourself

- Review what you have done in this Unit and prepare for the next Unit.

REVIEW: Browse the website for Unit 5.

PREVIEW: Browse the website for Unit 6.

PREPARE: Look at the activities in Unit 6.

ORGANIZE: Cut out this page and put it in the portfolio pocket.

Unit 6 Work and Play

How can we eat well, study well, exercise well, live well, and have good relationships?

Warm-up Everyone

1. Write six things you should do, and three things you should not do.
2. Write them on the 'post-its' on this page.
3. Choose one thing from each list that you will achieve this week.

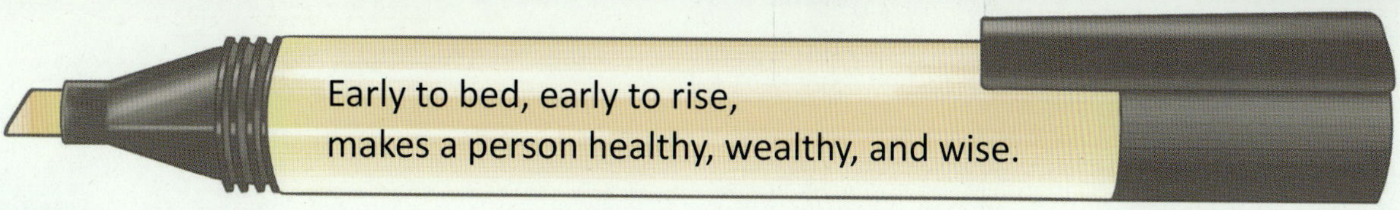

Pairs

- Talk about your 'to do' lists and your 'not to do' lists together.

*This Unit looks at spare time activities (speaking) and personal statements (writing).

Campus Friends: Traveling

Track 13

Emily loves Korea. The scenery and the weather are very different from her home in Nottingham.

Pairs

1. Look at the dialog together. The sentences are all mixed up.
2. Write the correct order of sentences in the right column.
3. Check the Glossary (▶ pages 147-154) for vocabulary.
4. Now read the dialog together.

Emily:	Hello, Deniz.	1
Deniz:	Have a great time.	
Emily:	I can study on the train.	
Deniz:	Really? You're not studying?	
Emily:	I thought I'd try Gyeongju.	
Deniz:	Hi, Emily. Long time no see.	2
Emily:	Thanks, I will.	
Deniz:	Great! You should visit Bulguksa and Seokguram.	
Emily:	I know. I went to Seoraksan last weekend.	
Deniz:	You're not kidding? How was your trip?	
Emily:	Fantastic! I'm traveling next weekend as well.	
Deniz:	Where are you going?	

*The correct version of this dialog is in the **Answer Section**, at the back of the book.

*There is another dialog about Emily's travels in the Word Bank (▶ page 135).

Pairs

- Make your own dialog about traveling.
- Perform it to another pair of classmates.

Reading: Work, Play, and Health

Track 14

Groups

Here is a magazine page about work and play. Read and discuss the articles together, especially the 'What do you think?' section. Check the vocabulary in the Word Bank.

FALL 2016

Work & Play

Why do we need to play?

When we think of living a healthy life, our thoughts usually turn to exercise, organic food, and regular sleep. However, there is another thing that is just as important - play. In fact, the United Nations has recognized it as a right of every child. The American Academy of Pediatrics states that play "contributes to the cognitive, physical, social, and emotional well-being of children and young people."

Despite these facts, our society has reduced the opportunities for play. On the one hand, people are moving to the cities (it is estimated that 70 percent of the world population will live in cities by 2050) and natural play areas are hard to find. On the other hand, today's hurried lifestyle, the increasing amount of schooling, and the attraction of sitting in front of the TV or the computer screen, mean that the amount of active, child-centered play is decreasing.

What do you think?

Zen proverb:
The secret to great work is great play.

Confucius:
Choose a job you love, and you will never have to work a day in your life.

George Sand:
Work is not man's punishment. It is his reward, his strength, and his pleasure.

Health is all!

A report by The University of Ulster indicates that children's play patterns can influence their health later in life. According to the study, adults who engaged in creative play as children were more likely to protect their health through eating a healthy diet and taking regular exercise.

In contrast, those who had less time to play as children were more likely to be overweight and have less healthy lifestyles.

When we lose our health, we find that it is the most valuable thing in the world. If active play leads to good health, then the real meaning of the proverb: 'All work and no play makes Jack a dull boy' becomes clear.

*There are more reading passages on the website: www.finchpark.com/KNUFLE/book-2/unit06/read.html.

Survey: Spare Time Activities

What do people like to do in their spare time? We can find out by conducting a survey.

Groups

1. Look at the survey in the tablet screen below.
2. Choose some activities (bottom of the page) and write them in the gaps.
3. Make questions for each item and ask everyone in the class.
   - Do you like watching movies and playing sports?
   - Can you speak French or Chinese?
4. Talk together about your results and enter them in the boxes 1. ☐ to 6. ☐.

1. How many people like both ________ and ________?
2. How many people like ________ but not ________?
3. How many people like not only ________ but also ________?
4. How many people like ________ better than ________?
5. How many people can speak either ________ or ________?
6. How many people can neither ________ nor ________?

1. ☐ 2. ☐ 3. ☐ 4. ☐ 5. ☐ 6. ☐

By yourself

- Exchange places with someone in another group.
- Explain your results to the people in your new group.

Extra activity

- What is the most popular activity in the class?
- What is the least popular activity in the class?

hiking	exercising	reading books	keeping a diary	surfing the Internet
cooking	swimming	watching TV	learning a language	chatting on the Internet
running	travelling	watching movies	listening to music	playing computer games
fishing	meditating	taking photos	talking with friends	walking to school
studying	playing sports	writing a blog	doing homework	giving a presentation

Language Workshop: Coordination and Parallelism

When we use a series of words in a sentence, this is called 'parallel structure.' It is useful for personal statements (▶ pages 56, 137). The words must have the same form. The sentences also use conjunctions such as 'both … and,' 'not only … but also,' 'as well as,' 'either or,' and 'neither … nor' (▶ page 54).

Pairs

- Look at sentences 1 to 5.
- Underline the series words that have the same form (adjective, noun, or verb).
- Highlight the conjunctions.

Home Layout Document Elements Tables Charts SmartArt Review

1. Our thoughts usually turn to healthy exercise, organic food and regular sleep. (▶ p. 53)
2. I am not only passionate, but also diligent, hard working, and responsible. (▶ p. 56)
3. This is causing pollution, deserts, and a lack of food. (▶ p. 56)
4. They told me about the need to recycle, make safe energy, and grow food. (▶ p. 56)
5. I am interested both in acupuncture and herbal medicine. (▶ p. 137)

Groups

- Look at sentences 6 to 12.
- Find the words in series and the conjunctions.
- Correct the mistakes together.

Home Layout Document Elements Tables Charts SmartArt Review

6. In my spare time, I enjoy reading, watching movies, and ~~to meet~~ meeting friends.
7. I hope to get a good job, contribute to the company, and making the most of my talents.
8. I hope not only to travel, but as well as experiencing other cultures.
9. I hope both to be a teacher and opening my own business.
10. Every morning I either go swimming and tennis.
11. I am applying for a summer internship in either Harvard as well as Stanford University.
12. I prefer teamwork than work by myself.

By yourself

- Write two sentences about yourself.
- Use conjunctions and words in series.

1. --

2. --

*The answers to the problems on this page are in the **Answer Section**, at the back of the book.
*Learn about coordination and parallelism on the website: www.finchpark.com/KNUFLE/book-2/unit06/.

Sample Personal Statement

Track 15

When applying for an internship, study abroad, or a graduate program, we often have to submit a personal statement. Here is Chang-min's personal statement. It is based on his short bio (▶page 123). Kadi's personal statement is on page 137 and there are more samples on www.finchpark.com/KNUFLE/book-2.

Groups

- Look at Chang-min's personal statement.
- Read it together and talk about it.

❶ Write about your ideas.

❷ Write about your qualities.

❸ Write about your personality.

❹ When did you decide on your major?

❺ Write about your family and your background.

❻ What makes you different from other people?

❼ What ideas are important to you?

❽ Write about special experiences. What did you learn from them?

❾ Write about your goals.

Personal Statement: Lee Chang-min

It is my dream to be an Earth Scientist and I want to follow this dream wherever it takes me. I am not only passionate, but also diligent, hard working, and responsible. I believe these qualities will help me to achieve my goals.

I became interested in Earth Sciences in high school. I learned that humans are using up the Earth's resources. This is causing pollution, deserts, and a lack of food. I decided then that I would help to make a sustainable world. My parents also influenced me. They told me about the need to recycle, make safe energy, and grow food for everyone on the planet.

Earth Sciences cover many aspects of life. I don't want to do the same thing all my life. I want to use all my skills and share all my talents. There are no simple solutions to the world's problems and I want to help in any way I can.

Baden-Powell, the leader of the Scouts, said, "Leave the world a little better than you found it." I really like this idea, and I want to apply it to my life. When I was in high school I was the editor of the class newspaper and I wrote about my ideas. I also played on the school tennis team. This helped me learn about teamwork and respect for other people's ideas.

While in university I have been trying to develop many skills. I am a member of the photography club and I have a computer certificate. I hope that my positive attitude and my belief in lifelong learning will help me to become a good person and a good scientist.

Introduction paragraph → Body paragraphs → Conclusion paragraph

Personal Statement: Checklist and Hints

Pairs

- Here is a personal statement checklist. Talk about these questions together.
- You will write your answers in your personal statement (▶pages 58, 59, and 60).

Question	Hint
1. What is special or interesting about me?	
2. Who has influenced me?	Family, friends, teachers, role models, etc.
3. What values and ideas are important to me?	Motto, proverb, quote, etc.
4. What is my personality?	My best qualities
5. What are my skills and achievements?	Responsibilities, hobbies, volunteering, prizes, sports
6. Have I had any big problems in my life?	How did I overcome them?
7. Have I had any special experiences?	What were they? What did I learn from them?
8. When and why did I decide my major?	
9. Have I had any special training?	Workshops, seminars, etc.
10. Why am I applying for this position?	▶Page 133, Q & A #17
11. What are my career goals?	▶Page 133, Q & A #20
12. What makes me a strong applicant?	▶Page 133, Q & A #18

By yourself

- Here are some more hints for writing your personal statement.

1. Make a list of ideas.
2. Make a clear outline.
3. Use plain text (no bold, underlining, or italics).
4. Make the opening paragraph interesting.
5. Show your motivation and enthusiasm.
6. Explain about your experience and knowledge.
7. Highlight and expand on your achievements.
8. Check the spelling and grammar.
9. Show your drafts to other people and ask for feedback.
10. Check the word count (250-300 words or one page).
11. Change your statement for each application.
12. Find out about the school or company.

*There are more personal statement tips and samples at www.finchpark.com/KNUFLE/book-2.

My Personal Statement: First Draft

You are applying for a job, graduate program, internship, etc., and you have to write a personal statement.

By yourself

- First of all, decide on the position you are applying for.
- Next, make an outline of what you will write in each paragraph.
- Check pages 56, 57, 137 and the website for samples and hints.
- Use your short bio (▶ page 19) and your autobiography (▶ page 39).

I am applying for: ______________________ at: ______________________

Home | Layout | Document Elements | Tables | Charts | SmartArt | Review

My personal statement: Outline

Introduction paragraph

____

____

Body paragraph 1

____

____

Body paragraph 2

____

____

Body paragraph 3

____

____

Conclusion paragraph

____

____

Peer-editing

- Discuss your outline with a classmate.
- Check spelling, grammar, and format together.
- Talk about your ideas. Have you included everything?

Personal Statement: Second Draft

By yourself

- Write your second draft, based on the feedback from your classmate.
- If you type it on a computer, print out the file and give it to the teacher.
- If you write it on this page, cut out this page and give it to the teacher for comments and feedback.
- Remember to add your name, student number, and date.

My Personal Statement: Final Draft

By yourself

- Rewrite or type your personal statement based on the feedback from your teacher.
- If you type it on a computer, print it out and put it in the portfolio pocket.
- Remember to print your name and write your signature.

Review

- Review what you have learned in this Unit and prepare for the next Unit.

Review:
Browse the website for Unit 6.

Prepare:
Look at the activities in Unit 7.

Preview:
Browse the website for Unit 7.

Organize:
Put your final draft in the portfolio pocket.

Unit 7 Think Smart

Everyone has a different mix of Multiple Intelligences (MIs). These eight intelligences help us to be good at different subjects and different jobs. What MI mix do you have?

Warm-up Everyone

1. Look at the pictures and titles on this page.
2. How smart do you think you are in each intelligence?
3. Mark your score (1 to 5) for each one.

Nature smart

1	2	3	4	5

People smart

1	2	3	4	5

Number smart

1	2	3	4	5

Picture/space smart

1	2	3	4	5

Self smart

1	2	3	4	5

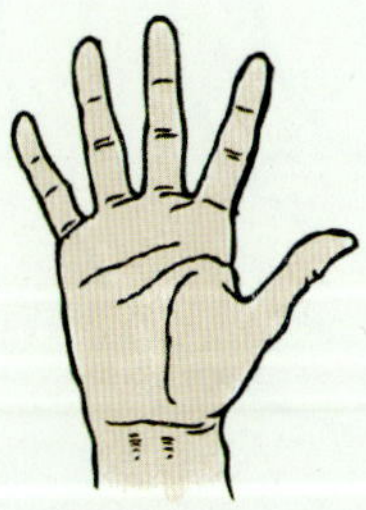

Body smart

1	2	3	4	5

Music smart

1	2	3	4	5

Word smart

1	2	3	4	5

Pairs

- Talk about your MI strengths and weaknesses together.
  - How nature-smart are you?
  - How number-smart are you?

*This Unit looks at Multiple Intelligences (speaking) and cover letters (writing).

Reading: Multiple Intelligences

Groups

1. Here is a magazine page about Multiple Intelligences.
2. Read the descriptions together and fill in your scores on the chart.
3. Talk about your MIs together (bottom of the page).

New Science Today

Special Issue: Multiple Intelligences - Are They Real?

What are your Multiple Intelligences? Fill in your scores on this page to find out.

Interpersonal

You notice the behavior and emotions of other people. You love to communicate with others and you learn best with others.

Musical/Rhythmic

You love rhythm and melody. You like to study with background music. Music helps you to learn new skills and ideas.

Bodily/Kinesthetic

You like to move and touch things. You are good with your body and with tools. You learn best through actions.

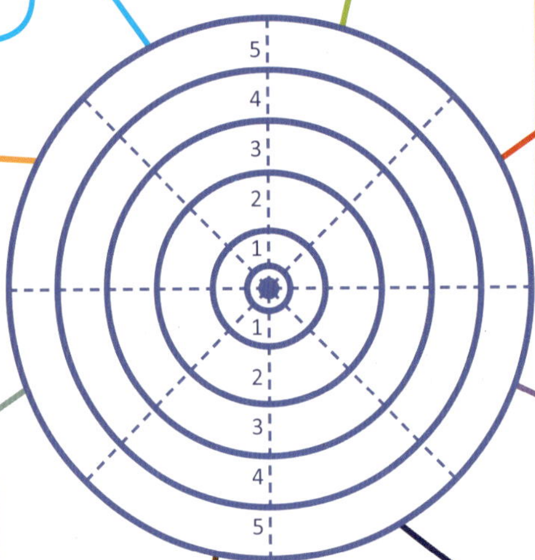

Visual/Spatial

You like to see things (pictures, graphs, charts, and tables) when you learn. Images are important to you.

Intrapersonal

You know your strengths, needs, and goals. You understand yourself and work best by yourself.

Logical/Mathematic

Organization is important to you. You love numbers and patterns. You like to learn in logical steps.

Naturalistic

You love nature and you care for the environment. For you, learning must happen freely and naturally.

Linguistic/Verbal

You love words and language. You like playing with words. You learn best by thinking about the words.

Discussion:

1. What is your strongest intelligence? What is your weakest intelligence?
2. How can we strengthen our weak intelligences?
3. Which intelligences does a doctor need? Why?
4. Which intelligences do you need for your major? Why?

Career Intelligences

Do you think certain Multiple Intelligences suit certain jobs?

Groups

1. Look at the name cards on this page.
2. Discuss the most suitable Multiple Intelligences for these jobs (▶ page 62).
3. Write the names of the MI types under the name cards.

*Suggested answers are in the **Answer Section**, at the back of the book.

Campus Friends: Giving Advice

Track 16

Whatever MIs we have, there is no substitute for hard work! Minghua has been given some advice about university life (work and play) by some senior students. He will share this advice with Ji-won and Kadi.

Groups

- Read and perform this short dialog together.
- Change roles and read it again.

Minghua:	Hello you two!
Ji-won:	You look happy. What have you been up to?
Minghua:	I've interviewed some senior students about school life.
Kadi:	That's a good idea. What did they say?
Minghua:	They had some very good advice for us freshmen.
Ji-won:	Don't keep it to yourself! What did they say?
Kadi:	Yes, come on. Spill the beans!
Minghua:	Well, first of all ... (fade out)

Groups

- You can see the advice on page 138.
- Use this advice to make a role-play between seniors and freshmen.
- There are useful phrases in the Word Bank (▶ pages 115 to 121).
- You can also use the words at the bottom of this page.

My notes for the role-play

Here are ten ways to thank the seniors for their advice.

1. I can never thank you enough.
2. Thanks. I hadn't thought of that.
3. I really appreciate your help.
4. I'm happy to learn from you.
5. Thank you for telling me this.
6. Thank you for your advice.
7. Thank you for your kindness.
8. You're very kind.
9. That sounds like a great idea.
10. That's really helpful.

Cover Letter: Unscramble

When we apply for a job, graduate school, or internship, we need to send a cover letter with the résumé. Here is a sample cover letter, but everything is in the wrong order. Can you sort it out?

Groups

1. Read the cover letter on this page together.
2. Discuss the order of paragraphs and other contents (date, name, etc.).
3. Write the number of each item in the circle on the left.

Personnel Department
American Pacific Foodstuffs
123 Dangeun Gil, Kangbuk-gu
Seoul 010-101

Ji-won Moon
608 Moojigae APT.
Gyeongju, 780-900

◯ Ji-won Moon

◯ While at university, I participated in the guitar club. I also received cooking certificates and taught Korean to foreigners. These activities, which I participated in regularly, have broadened my cultural understanding.

◯ Dear Sir/Madam,

◯ I am 24 years old and my degree, which is in food nutrition, is from Kyungpook National University. I have studied English in Indonesia, and I have been an exchange student in Europe. I also have an IELTS certificate (score: 7.5).

◯ 010-123-4567

◯ If appointed, I could communicate effectively with clients living around the world. I am single and willing to travel as part of the job.

◯ *Ji-won Moon*

◯ I hope to have the opportunity to talk about my application. I am free any time for an interview, and I look forward to meeting you.

◯ Yours sincerely,

◯ My personality, which is calm and friendly, helps me to work with people. My motto, which I feel makes me a good applicant, is 'Cleanliness is half of health.'

◯ Thank you for your time.

◯ With reference to your job advertisement on the asiajobs59.com website, I would like to apply for the position of assistant food advisor in your export department.

(1) April 20, 2017

*There is a suggested answer in the **Answer Section**, at the back of the book.

Language Workshop: Relative Clauses

When we write a cover letter, relative clauses help us to say things briefly. This makes it easier to keep the length of the cover letter to one page. Relative clauses are explained on page 139.

Pairs

- Look at the sentences in the boxes below. Talk about them together.
- Combine the two sentences in each box, using *who*, *which*, *where*, or *that*.
- Look at page 139 if you need help.

My degree is in food nutrition. My degree is from Kyungpook National University.

____ (▸ page 65)

I graduated from Kyungpook National University. I was on the university basketball team.

____

____ (▸ page 67)

I participated in these activities regularly. They helped my cultural understanding.

____

____ (▸ page 65)

My philosophy will help me contribute to Atlantic Engineering. My philosophy is that hard work brings success.

____

____ (▸ page 67)

My motto makes me a good applicant. My motto is 'Cleanliness is half of health'.

____ (▸ page 65)

The Nobel Prize in Physics for 2010 was given to Andre Geim and Konstantin Novoselov. Andre Geim and Konstantin Novoselov were professors at the University of Manchester.

____

____

*The answers for the tasks on this page are in the **Answer Section**, at the back of the book.

Sample Email Cover Letter

Track 17

We can write a hard copy cover letter or send it by email. Minghua is sending his cover letter with his application form and résumé. You can also see Emily's story-based cover letter on page 141.

Groups

1. Read Minghua's cover letter together. Talk about the format and the content.
2. Write a description of each part of the email in the boxes on the right of the page.
3. Look at page 140 for help and suggestions.

To: personel@atlantic.com

Subject: Application for internship with Atlantic Engineering: Zhang

Attach a file | Receipt On Read : ☐ | Receipt On Delivery : ☐

Cc | Bcc | Signature | Addresses | Save Draft | Send | Check Spelling

Internship Application Reference Number: XYZ123456

Dear Ms. Janice Spoonby,

Please find attached my application form, résumé, and certificates, which are required according to the job announcement on the website of your company.

I am applying for this internship because I think I am the kind of person who would fit in well with your company. I have an outgoing personality and experience of working with people.

I recently graduated with a degree in International Trade from Kyungpook National University, where I was a member of the university basketball team. My philosophy, which is that hard work brings success, will help me contribute to Atlantic Engineering as an active member of the Marketing Department.

During my time in university, I participated in various student clubs and studied English, Korean, and Japanese, in addition to my mother tongue (Chinese). These activities have helped me prepare for a career in marketing.

I would welcome an opportunity to talk with you about my application. My goal is to study for an MBA and an internship in your company would be a great start.

Thank you for your time.

Yours sincerely,

Minghua Zhang

757 Chong-ro
Dongseo-gu 135, Nam-dong
Daegu 704-789
053-987-6543; mzhang@hmail.com

Application-Zhang.pdf
Resume-Zhang.pdf

1.

2.

3.

4.

5.

6.

7.

8.

9.

10.

11.

12.

My Cover Letter: First Draft

Now it's your chance to write an email cover letter. First of all, decide what you are applying for.

☐ Full-time job ☐ Internship abroad ☐ Graduate study abroad
☐ Exchange student position ☐ Other

By yourself

- Brainstorm what to include in the email.
- Write your first draft (▶ pages 67, 140, 141, 159).

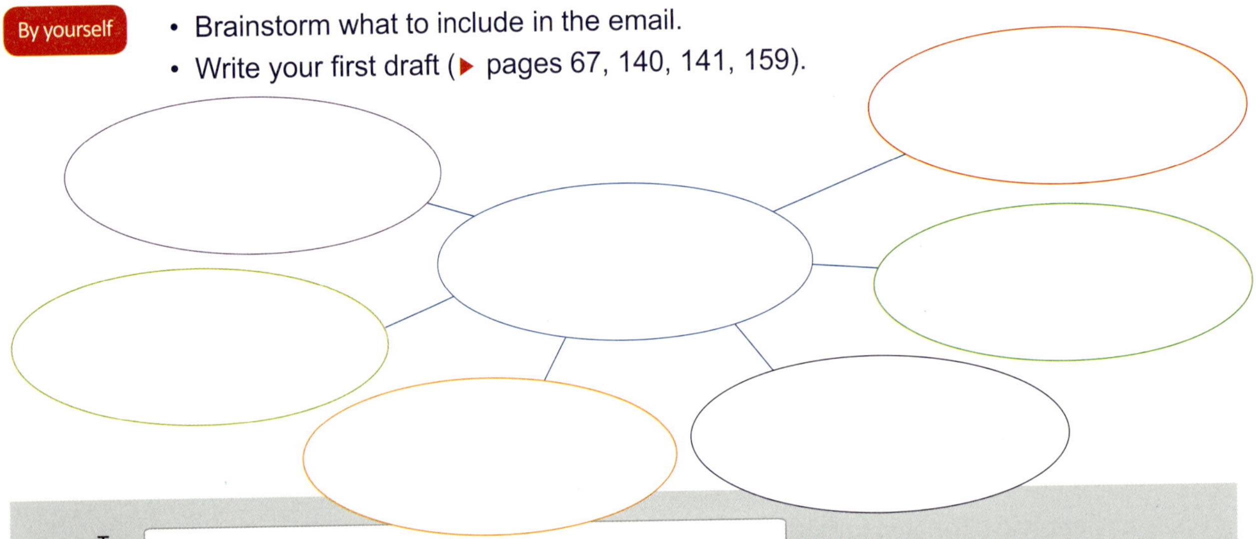

To
Subject
Attach a file Receipt On Read : ☐ Receipt On Delivery : ☐
Cc Bcc Signature Addresses Save Draft Send Check Spelling

My Cover Letter: Final Draft

Before you write your final draft, you need to self/peer-edit the first draft with a classmate.

Pairs

- Ask a classmate to look at your first draft (▶ page 68).
- Edit the draft together. Look at pages 65/159, 67/140, and 141, for form and content.
- Look at the Marking Code (▶ page 122) for grammar and paragraph style.

By yourself

- Rewrite your cover letter based on the self/peer-editing.
- If you type the final draft, stick it on this page or put it in the portfolio pocket.

To ______________________________

Subject ______________________________

Attach a file　Receipt On Read : ☐　Receipt On Delivery : ☐

Cc　Bcc　Signature　Addresses　Save Draft　Send　Check Spelling

Self-assessment: My Writing Skills

What level are your writing skills? How can you improve them? This self-assessment is based on the European Council's DIALANG.

By yourself

- Read the sentences below, and check (✓) the statements that apply to you.
- What is your writing level?

LEVEL	Self-assessment statements: Writing	✓
A1	I can write simple notes to friends.	
A1	I can describe where I live.	
A1	I can fill in forms with personal details.	
A1	I can write simple phrases and sentences.	
A2	I can write short, basic descriptions of events.	
A2	I can write short notes and messages about everyday life.	
A2	I can write about my family, home, or school.	
A2	I can write about my opinions, plans, and actions.	
B1	I can write about experiences, feelings, and events.	
B1	I can describe dreams, hopes, and ambitions.	
B1	I can write about a book or film and add my reactions.	
B1	I can write short, information-based reports.	
B2	I can write about different solutions to a problem.	
B2	I can summarize information and arguments.	
B2	I can write an essay that follows a logical line of argument.	
B2	I can write about cause and effect, results, and possibilities.	

By yourself

- Review what you have done in this Unit and prepare for the next Unit.

Review:
Browse the website for Unit 7.

Prepare:
Look at the activities in Unit 8.

Preview:
Browse the website for Unit 8.

Organize:
Cut out this page and put it in the portfolio pocket.

Unit 8 That's Entertainment!

What was your favorite entertainment when you were a child? Has it changed?

By yourself

- Look at the entertainment survey on this page.
- Fill in your past favorites and your current favorites.

ENTERTAINMENT SURVEY (1)

When I was a child	Now I am an adult
1. My favorite book was:	My favorite book is:
2. My favorite song was:	My favorite song is:
3. My favorite TV show was:	My favorite TV show is:
4. My favorite sportsperson was:	My favorite sportsperson is:
5. My favorite music was:	My favorite music is:
6. My favorite movie was:	My favorite movie is:
7. My favorite actor was:	My favorite actor is:

Pairs

- Talk with a classmate about your survey results.
- Try to use 'Compare and contrast' phrases (▶ page 118) and 'Expressing surprise' phrases (▶ page 119).

No entertainment is so cheap as reading, nor any pleasure so lasting.
(Mary Worley Montagu)

We aren't in an information age. We are in an entertainment age.
(Anthony Robbins)

*This Unit looks at entertainment (speaking) and book/movie/restaurant reviews (writing).

Campus Friends: Sport

Track 18

Deniz and Chang-min are talking about a soccer game between Korea and Turkey. However, Emily likes women's soccer.

Groups

- Read and perform this dialog together.
- Change roles and read it again.
- Check unfamiliar words in the Glossary (▶pages 147-154).

Deniz:	Hi, Chang-min. Did you see the match last night?
Chang-min:	Of course! Did you cheer for both teams?
Deniz:	Well, at first I was on the side of Turkey, but then ...
Chang-min:	You started cheering for Korea?
Deniz:	Yes, when the referee disallowed Korea's goal!
Chang-min:	The video replay showed it wasn't offside.
Deniz:	That's right! I really don't like unfair decisions.
Chang-min:	Even the commentators said it was a goal.
Deniz:	Sure, but the referee wouldn't change his mind.
Emily:	Hello, you two. Are you talking about men's soccer again?
Deniz:	What do you mean, men's soccer?
Emily:	Didn't you know? I used to play women's soccer in England.
Chang-min:	That's fantastic! Why don't we have a game today?
Emily:	I'd love to, but I've got a movie review to write.
Deniz:	Maybe next time.

Discussion

1. Do you prefer to play sports or watch other people play them? Why?
2. Can you remember any wrong decisions made by referees? Talk about them.
3. Is sport entertainment?
4. What do you think about the Olympics? How about the Paralympics?

Reading: Entertainment

Track 19

Groups

1. Here is a magazine page about entertainment.
2. Read the articles together and ask each other the "Discuss" questions.
3. Check unfamiliar vocabulary in the Glossary (▶pages 147-154).

Entertainment: Active or Passive?

Imagine sitting at home on a Sunday afternoon, two hundred years ago. What will you do with your free time? You can't turn on the radio, watch cable TV or online music videos, or talk with your best friend on your smartphone. You can't even catch a bus, take a train, or drive to a national park.

On the other hand, you can read a book, write a letter, play a musical instrument, sing, go for a walk, play chess, or do some drawing or painting. These are all active forms of self-entertainment. They build the mind and the body.

In contrast, 21st century entertainment is mostly passive. Rather than picking up a violin, we are more likely to listen to a CD-ROM or mp3. Rather than joining a soccer team, we are more likely to watch soccer on television. Rather than reading a book, we are more likely to watch a DVD.

Are we as active in our entertainment as people were 200 years ago, or are we passive observers? Is entertainment about using our talents, or is it just a way of filling in the time?

Discuss

1. What do you do in your spare time?
2. Is it good for babies to watch television?
3. What is the purpose of entertainment?
4. Can you entertain yourself without smart technology?
5. What are the advantages and disadvantages of the Internet?
6. Do movies reflect life, or does life reflect movies?

The Wonder of Childhood

Technology has changed the nature of entertainment. The average American child or teenager spends almost eight hours a day playing video games, watching TV, or surfing the Internet. Because of this, we need to ask whether computer games and movies reflect life, or vice versa.

Research tells us that society takes its values from film and television. This is a big problem for parents who want their children to experience the wonder of childhood.

Passive entertainment is not good for babies, either. Sitting them in front of a television might keep them quiet, but it takes time away from exploring the things around them, learning motor skills, and acquiring language.

Entertainment Survey (2)

Here is another entertainment survey. This time you will collect information from other people.

By yourself

- Choose SET 1, SET 2, SET 3, or SET 4 (below).
- Ask the questions in your SET to four people.
- Write their answers in the Q & A boxes.

SET 1 (Television)

1. Do you like TV mini-series?
2. Do you like documentaries?
3. Do you like comedy shows?
4. Do you like reality shows?
5. Do you watch TV news?
6. Do you watch quiz shows?
7. Do you watch sports on TV?

SET 2 (Music and Stage)

1. Can you play a musical instrument?
2. Have you ever been to a live concert?
3. Have you ever watched a stage play?
4. Would you like to be a singer?
5. Would you like to be a musician?
6. Would you like to be an actor?
7. Would you like to be a DJ?

SET 3 (Reading)

1. Do you read novels?
2. Do you read magazines?
3. Do you read newspapers?
4. Do you read self-help books?
5. Would you like to write a book?
6. Do you read news on the Internet?
7. Do you have a Facebook page?

SET 4 (Movies)

1. Do you like historical movies?
2. Do you like action movies?
3. Do you like romantic comedies?
4. Do you like horror movies?
5. Do you like spy movies?
6. Do you like SCI-FI movies?
7. Would you like to be a movie star?

Q & A Boxes

Qs	Person 1 answers	Person 2 answers	Person 3 answers	Person 4 answers
1.				
2.				
3.				
4.				
5.				
6.				
7.				

By yourself → Groups

- Find the people who asked the same SET of questions as you.
- Talk about your results and analyze them together.

Everybody says that:	
Most people say that:	
Some people say that:	
Very few people say that:	
Nobody says that:	

This activity is based on *It's Up to You*. Finch & Sampson (2004), pages 120, 121.

Language Workshop: Active/passive

The active voice tells us what the subject of a sentence does. The passive voice tells us what is done to the subject. This can be useful for describing the work of authors, actors, directors, and chefs, when we write book reviews, movie reviews, or restaurant reviews.

Groups

1. Look at the board game on this page. All the sentences are in the active voice.
2. When you land on a square, say the sentence in the passive voice.
3. For example: 'Ms. Page wrote the book.' ➡ *The book was written by Ms. Page.*

START HERE.

Ms. Page wrote the book.

Hannah played the princess.

Brett acted the main character.

GO FORWARD 3 SPACES.

I ate the cheese pizza.

Jimmy directed the movie.

The waitress cleaned the table.

I read the book.

I finished the assignment.

He wrote the first draft.

GO BACK TO THE START.

They released the movie yesterday.

The waiter served the meal.

They published the book in 2013.

MISS THE NEXT TURN.

She sang the song beautifully.

Many people saw the movie.

He downloaded the ebook.

The author won the Pulitzer Prize.

GO BACK 2 SPACES.

She paid for the meal.

The movie won many awards.

ROLL AGAIN.

I didn't do my homework.

Peter Quin produced the film.

The mayor opened the restaurant.

I paid the bill.

The player kicked the ball.

Sam Jin wrote the screenplay.

I bought the book.

I lost my pen.

FINISH!

Sample Reviews

Track 20

When you want to find out about a movie, a book, or a restaurant, you can read a review. The reviews on this page will help you make the outlines on page 77 and the drafts on pages 78 and 79.

Pairs

- Read the reviews on this page together.
- Check the Glossary (▶ pages 147-154) for unfamiliar words.
- How many passive verbs can you find? (▶ Word Bank, Answer Section)

"The Tree" was directed by Jimmy Wood, based on the book by Simon Oak. The main characters are played by Paul Bark, Justin Birch, and Leaf Malone. In this movie, two friends meet under a tree that has been dead for years. As the film goes on, the friends become lovers and the tree comes to life again. The movie is optimistic, and the acting is sincere and warm-hearted. I liked the scene in which the tree comes to life, but I didn't like the music. It should be more romantic.

"Out of Time" was written by Justa Minute in 2013. It is set in 2050 and 1600. In the novel, a strange, backward clock is found by a young girl. When she moves the hands on the clock, she is taken back to England in 1600. She discovers that the history books are wrong about Shakespeare and Queen Elizabeth, but when she returns to 2050, no one believes her. This is a gripping read. I liked the idea of finding the truth about history, but I didn't like the ending. It was a little boring and confusing.

Mizzo's restaurant was opened last week by the famous Italian singer, Mucho di Pasta. The restaurant is located in the town center, opposite the Arts Center. All the dishes on the menu are prepared by an Italian chef, and they are brought to your table by cheerful, friendly waiters. I liked the pineapple pizza and the comfortable atmosphere, but I wasn't too happy about the loud music. All in all, if you like Italian food, this is a must-visit eating-place for you and your friends.

Writing a Review: Outlining

Pairs

- Think about a good movie, book, or restaurant.
- Fill in the review outlines on this page. Discuss them together.
- There are lots of useful adjectives in the Word Bank (▶ page 114).

Movie title:		
Director:		
Main actors:		
Plot:		
Your opinion	This movie is:	
	The acting is:	
	I liked:	
	I didn't like:	
Recommendation:		

Book title:		
Author:		
Genre:		
Plot:		
Your opinion	This book is:	
	The story is:	
	I liked:	
	I didn't like:	
Recommendation:		

Restaurant name:		
Type of food:		
Main dishes:		
Location:		
Your opinion	This place is:	
	The food is:	
	I liked:	
	I didn't like:	
Recommendation:		

My Review: First Draft

By yourself

- Choose one of your outlines on page 77.
- Think of more things you can say about the book/movie/restaurant.
- Write a review for a magazine. This is your first draft.

Magazine name:

Review title:

logo

picture

Write your name and the date:

Pairs

- Edit your first draft with a classmate.
- Look for grammar, paragraph format (▶page 122), and content (ideas).

My Review: Final Draft

By yourself

- Rewrite your review, based on the peer-editing on page 78.
- If you type your final draft, stick it on this page or put it in the portfolio pocket.

Self-assessment: My Listening Skills

How are your listening skills? How can you improve them? This self-assessment is based on the European Council's DIALANG.

By yourself

- Read the sentences below and check (✓) the statements that apply to you.
- What is your listening level?

LEVEL	Self-assessment statements: Listening	✓
A1	I can understand simple, clear, repeated speech.	
A1	I can follow slow speech with long pauses.	
A1	I can understand instructions and short, simple directions.	
A1	I can understand numbers, prices, and times.	
A2	I can understand enough to meet my needs in everyday life.	
A2	I can do simple business in shops, post offices, or banks.	
A2	I can identify the main point of TV news items.	
A2	I can find the main point in simple messages and announcements.	
B1	I can follow clear, everyday conversation.	
B1	I can follow a lecture if the topic is familiar.	
B1	I can follow films in which the story is simple and the language is clear.	
B1	I can catch the main points in broadcasts on familiar topics.	
B2	I can understand standard spoken language.	
B2	I can follow lectures, talks, and reports, which use complex language.	
B2	I can understand messages and announcements at normal speed.	
B2	I can understand TV news, current affairs programs, and most films.	

By yourself

- Review what you have done in this Unit and prepare for the next Unit.

REVIEW: Browse the website for Unit 8.

PREVIEW: Browse the website for Unit 9.

PREPARE: Look at the activities in Unit 9.

ORGANIZE: Put this page in the portfolio pocket.

Unit 9 Drama Project

Drama develops reading, writing, speaking, and listening skills. It also helps you to use non-verbal communication (gestures, body language). Let's begin this drama project with some theatre games.

Pairs

1. THE MIRROR

- **Students A and B:** Stand opposite each other, face to face.
- **Student A:** You are looking in a mirror.
  - Don't say anything.
  - Make actions with your face, arms, and body.
- **Student B**: You ARE the mirror.
  - Copy Student A's actions exactly.
- Change roles.

Purpose: to help you think about your whole body.

Pairs

2. THE LIVING STATUE

- **Students A and B:** You are going to make a statue.
  - Decide what your statue will be.
  - Decide where your statue will be placed.
- **Student A:** You ARE the statue.
  - Stand up and stay still.
  - Don't say anything. Listen to Student B.
  - Follow student B's instructions.
- **Student B**: You are the sculptor.
  - Give directions to Student A.
  - "Raise your arm. Lower your head."
  - "Up a bit. Down a bit. Hold it there."

- **Student B:** Walk around the room. Look at all the statues.
  - Which statue is the most creative?

Purposes: 1) to help you think of the whole body; 2) to help you give and follow directions.

These games were adapted from *Theater Games for the Classroom*, by Viola Spolin (2000).

Drama is life with the dull bits cut out. (Alfred Hitchcock)

*In this Unit, your group will write a drama (writing) and perform it (speaking).
*There are more theatre games on this EFL drama site: www.finchpark.com/drama/tgames.html.

Campus Friends: Drama

Track 21

Four of the friends are talking about drama. If you check Kadi's short bio (▶ page 125), you can see that she was in the English Drama Club at her Gymnasium, in Tallinn.

Groups

- Read and perform this dialog together.
- Change roles and read it again.
- Check unfamiliar words in the Glossary (▶pages 147-154).

Emily: Hello Kadi. What are you looking at?

Kadi: It's my e-book reader.

Ji-won: What are you reading?

Kadi: It's a play by Shakespeare, called "As You Like It."

Minghua: Why don't we read it together?

Kadi: O.K. I'll start: "All the world's a stage,"

Emily: "And all the men and women merely players:"

Ji-won: "They have their exits and their entrances;"

Minghua: "And one man in his time plays many parts,"

Kadi: "His acts being seven ages."

Emily: Wow! That's amazing!

Ji-won: What does it mean to you, Minghua?

Minghua: It's about life. The world is a theater.

Kadi: Yes, and we act many roles in that theater.

Emily: Children, parents, business-people, grandparents, ...

Ji-won: I love drama. Shall we read it again?

Groups

- **Puzzle time:** Kadi mentions the seven ages of man.
- Can you match these seven ages with the pictures below?

Second childhood
Judge
Soldier
School child
Infant
Lover
Old age

*The answer is in the **Answer Section**, at the back of the book.

Action Stories

Here are some action stories that will help you develop your acting skills.

Groups

- **Storyteller:** Read the scripts slowly. Pause after each line.
- **Actors:** Perform the actions after the storyteller pauses. Use your whole body.

Action Story 1: The Dream

Storyteller	Actors
1. A man was lost in a forest.	1. Walk around. Look. Search.
2. It got dark.	2. You can't see anything. Listen.
3. Then it got cold.	3. Be cold! Use all your body.
4. Then it rained.	4. Be wet! Use your coat as an umbrella.
5. Then the wind blew strongly.	5. Fight against the wind.
6. Then he fell and broke his arm.	6. Fall over. Hold your arm. It's painful!
7. A tree fell on him, breaking his legs.	7. Hold your legs. It really hurts. Scream!
8. Then he heard wolves coming.	8. Listen. Oh no! Use all your body.
9. Finally, he awoke. He had been dreaming.	9. Wake up. Be surprised. Be happy!

Action Story 2: Mrs. Jones

Storyteller	Actors
1. Mrs. Jones walked with a stick. She was 80.	1. Walk slowly, with a stick.
2. I used to carry her shopping bags for her.	2. Carry some shopping bags.
3. One day, she bought a bottle of medicine.	3. Make the shape of a bottle.
4. She slowly climbed the steps to her house.	4. Hobble slowly up the steps.
5. The next time I saw her, she was walking with no stick. She waved to me.	5. Walk with a straight back. Wave.
6. The next time we met she was sitting on a bench in the park. She looked 40.	6. Sit on a bench. Look happy.
7. The next week she looked 20. I held her hand and asked her for a date.	7. Take someone's hand.
8. I waited, but she didn't show up for the date.	8. Wait. Look at your watch.
9. I went to her home and knocked on the door.	9. Walk quickly. Knock loudly.
10. There was no answer.	10. Wait. Look sad.

Drama Board Game

Groups

- Play this drama board game together.
- When you land on a drama icon, choose a card on page 85. Talk about it.

*This game is adapted from *It's Up to You!*, Finch & Sampson, 2004, pp. 102-3.

Drama Board Game: Icon Cards

Groups

- Each card can only be used one time.
- Cross the card out when it has been used.

What is the *script*?	What does *exit, stage left* mean? (stage directions)	What is the difference between comedy and tragedy?	Would you rather be an actor or a director? Why?
What is the difference between *monologue* and *dialogue*?	Name three Korean folktales. Talk about them.	What is the *Green Room*? (stage-term)	Name three fairy tales. Talk about them.
What is your favorite TV mini-series? Why?	What do *downstage* and *backstage* mean?	Name three Aesop fables. Talk about them	'Drama is life.' Do you agree? Why? Why not?
What is the difference between an *Act* and a *Scene*?	What does *Hollywood ending* mean?	What is a *trapdoor*? What is it used for?	What does *break a leg* mean?
Would you like to be an actor? Why? Why not?	What is a *dress rehearsal*?	Have you seen a stage play? Talk about it.	Have you ever acted in a play? Talk about it.
Talk about a Korean Mask Dance.	Who is your favorite actor? Why?	What is the *cast* of a play?	What is the *final curtain*?
Name one of Shakespeare's tragedies.	What is a *stage direction*? Give some examples.	What are *props*? Give some examples.	Name one of Shakespeare's historical plays.

*This game is adapted from *It's Up to You!*, Finch & Sampson, 2004, pp. 102-3.

Role-Plays

Groups

Here is a role-play for you to perform in your groups. There are more role-play situations in the Word Bank (▶pages 142-144).

International Marriage — Role A: Young person

Situation: You are in love with a foreigner and you want to marry him/her. You will tell your parents of this decision today and ask for their approval. You feel that in this marriage, you will:

1. Develop a broader point-of-view
2. Share cultural backgrounds
3. Have a chance to travel or live overseas
4. Raise bilingual children

You will speak first. "Mother (or Father), I have decided to marry a man (or woman) from (*name of country*). I hope that you will give your approval."

International Marriage — Role B: Mother

Situation: Your son/daughter wants to marry a foreigner. He/she is very happy with his/her international boy/girlfriend, and you want to help him/her. You don't mind if there will be problems. You just want him/her to be happy.

1. Talk to your son/daughter, along with the boy/girlfriend and your husband.
2. Explain your opinion and listen to the others' opinions.
3. Have a discussion about the situation. Make a decision together.

International Marriage — Role C: Father

Situation: Your son/daughter wants to marry a foreigner. You don't agree with international marriages. You want your Korean ancestral bloodline to continue. You feel that your son/daughter hasn't really thought about the problems. Where will they live? Where will your grandchildren go to school?

1. Talk to your son/daughter, along with the boy/girlfriend and your wife.
2. Explain your opinion and listen to the others' opinions.
3. Have a discussion about the situation. Make a decision together.

International Marriage — Role D: Girlfriend/Boyfriend

Situation: You are the girlfriend/boyfriend of a young Korean person. You really love each other and you want to get married. You understand that there are cultural problems, but you want to solve them. You want to be friends with the parents and a good son/daughter-in-law.

1. Talk to your boy/girlfriend's parents, along with your boy/girlfriend.
2. Explain your opinion and listen to the others' opinions.
3. Have a discussion about the situation. Make a decision together.

Theatre Games - Writing

On page 81, you did some theatre games (miming and speaking). There are two more theatre games on this page, but they are writing-based.

3. KIDNAP CLUES

By yourself

- On a piece of paper, make a list of 10 personal things.
- If you were kidnapped, a detective would find these things in your room.
- Give your list to the teacher.

Pairs

- The teacher will give you two lists made by two other people.
- Talk about these lists together.
- Who do you think wrote these lists?
- Interview the people whom you suspect made the lists.

Purpose: to help you develop your observation skills and your inferring skills.

4. SPLIT EXCHANGES

By yourself

- The teacher will give you a line of a script.
- Memorize your line.
- Walk around the room and say your line to other people.

Everyone

- Make a row of everyone in the room.
- The person at the front of the row has line number 1.
- The next person has line number 2. ....
- Perform the script by saying your lines one after the other.

Purposes: 1) to help you examine a drama script; 2) to help you write your own script.

These games were adapted from *Drama Techniques in Language learning*, by Alan Maley and Alan Duff, (2004).

*You can see the complete "Split Exchanges" script in the Word Bank (▶ page 135).

*There are more theatre games on this EFL drama site: www.finchpark.com/drama/tgames.html.

Finish the Story

Here are some folk stories from different cultures. This activity helps you to write a script. First make a plot by arranging the sentences and then write your own ending.

Pairs

- Read the sentences together and put them in order (1, 2, 3, ...).
- Talk about the story and write your own ending.

The Teacher's Jar (Korea)

	One day, a friend came to see him. He told the students to work hard until he returned.
	He said, "Do not touch this jar. If you taste what is inside, you will die at once."
1	Once upon a time, there was a traditional Korean school.
	As soon as he left, they began to play. One trainee suggested that they look in the jar.
	The teacher was a greedy, stern, unkind old man with a moustache.
	A few minutes later, he returned holding a jar.
	A few days later, he had to leave hastily, so he told the students to do homework.
	When they opened it, they noticed that the jar was full of ....
	(our ending)

Doctor Blue (Hungary)

	Doctor Blue owned a large apartment with many rooms.
	After the honeymoon, she gave the musician all the keys to their apartment.
	Doctor Blue had to go to a conference, leaving the musician in the apartment.
	Finally, he decided to look in the room his wife had told him not to.
	She got married to a young pop musician.
	That weekend, he looked in all the rooms except one.
	The doctor told him he could look in any room except one.
	When he opened the door ....
	(our ending)

*You can see suggested answers in the **Answer Section**, at the back of the book.

*There are more cultural stories in the Word Bank (▶ page 145).

Project Ideas

Groups It's time to decide on the topic for your mini-drama. Look at these ideas and talk about them. Do you want to use one of these ideas, or do you want to try something different?

1. Choose a traditional Korean folktale for your drama (See the ideas on the next page). The teacher can give you feedback on your writing.
    - Write the script.
    - Assign roles.
    - Learn your lines.
    - Rehearse the drama.
    - Prepare the costumes and props.

2. Choose an Aesop fable or a foreign folktale. (See the ideas on the next page). The teacher can give you feedback on your writing.
    - Write the script.
    - Assign roles.
    - Learn your lines.
    - Rehearse the drama.
    - Prepare the costumes and props.

3. Think of an important moment in history. This could be an important scientific discovery, a famous battle, or a famous love story, etc. The teacher can give you feedback on your writing.
    - Write the script.
    - Assign roles.
    - Learn your lines.
    - Rehearse the drama.
    - Prepare the costumes and props.

4. Create your own drama topic. You can base it on a TV mini-series if you want to. What will happen in your drama? Where? When? Will it be funny or serious? Will it have a moral? The teacher can give you feedback on your writing.
    - Write the script.
    - Assign roles.
    - Learn your lines.
    - Rehearse the drama.
    - Prepare the costumes and props.

Choosing a Story

Groups

Here are some ideas for your mini-drama. When you have made your final choice, brainstorm your ideas at the bottom of the page. Then make a plan of your drama on the next page (▶page 91).

Folktales and Aesop fables

KOREAN FOLKTALES	AESOP FABLES
Kongji-Patji: 콩쥐팥쥐	The Stork and the Fox
The Shim Choeng Story: 심청전	The Donkey and the Grasshopper
The Heongbu Nolbu Brothers: 흥부놀부전	The Ants and the Grasshopper
The Sun and the Moon: 해님달님	The Father and His Sons
The Jangwha Hongryon Story: 장화홍련전	The Kingdom of the Lion
The Chunhyang Story: 춘향전	The Musical Fisherman
The Mud Snail Bride: 우렁이 각시	The Thirsty Pigeon
The Gold Axe & Silver Axe: 금도끼 은도끼	The Wolf and the Dog
The Filial Tiger: 효자호랑이	The Three Pigs
The Rabbit and the Turtle: 별주부전	The Three Bears
The Hahoe Mask Drama: 하회 별신굿 탈놀이	Town Mouse/Country Mouse

Famous stories and TV dramas

FAMOUS STORIES	TV DRAMAS
Romeo and Juliet	The Moon Embracing the Sun: 해를 품은 달
Alice in Wonderland	My Princess: 마이 프린세스
Beauty and the Beast	Rooftop Prince: 옥탑방 왕세자
Little Red Riding Hood	The Princess's Man: 공주의 남자
The Three Kingdoms	Shut Up! Flower Boy Band: 닥치고 꽃미남밴드
Snow White and the Seven Dwarves	Dream High 2: 드림하이 2

Brainstorm your ideas for the title and topic and make notes here.

Project Planning

Groups

Now that you have decided on the title and topic for your mini-drama, you can start planning. Use this page to make a plan of action for everyone in your group.

Title:		
Roles:	Name:	Role(s):
	Name:	Role(s):
	Name:	Role(s):
	Name:	Role(s):
	Name:	Role(s):
Scenes:	1.	
	2.	
	3.	
	4.	
	5.	
	6.	
Props:		
Music:		
Other:	[Contact numbers, meeting times, etc.]	

Mini-drama: Storyboards

Groups

- Make an outline of your mini-drama, using these storyboards.

Mini-drama: First Draft

Groups

- Write the first draft of your mini-drama on this page.
- Ask the teacher for more paper if you need it.
- Talk with your group members and give as many ideas as you can. Be creative!

Mini-drama: Second Draft

Groups

- Show the first draft of your mini-drama to the teacher, for feedback.
- Write your second draft, based on this feedback.
- Underline your part, so that you can practice and memorize your words.

Mini-drama: Peer-assessment

By yourself

- Watch the mini-dramas of the other groups and assess each group on this page.
- **5 = Yes, absolutely. 4 = Yes. 3 = OK, so-so. 2 = Not really. 1 = Oh dear!**
- Add your comments about each group's drama and the members' performance.

MINI-DRAMAS: PEER-ASSESSMENT		Group ___	Group ___	Group ___	Group ___
1.	The drama took a reasonable amount of time.				
2.	The drama was well prepared.				
3.	The drama was well organized.				
4.	The drama was well written and easy to understand.				
5.	The drama was well performed.				
6.	The drama was enjoyable.				
7.	The drama was creative.				
8.	The drama was interesting.				
9.	The actors contributed equally.				
10.	The actors used expressive body language.				
11.	The actors were confident and cheerful.				
12.	Props and audio/visual effects were well made.				
	Total/60				

My comments

Group

Group

Group

Group

Mini-drama: Self-assessment

By yourself

- Think about your mini-drama and assess yourself on this page.
- **5 = Yes, absolutely. 4 = Yes. 3 = OK, so-so. 2 = Not really. 1 = Oh dear!**
- Add your comments about the drama and your performance.

MINI-DRAMA: SELF-ASSESSMENT		5	4	3	2	1
1.	I contributed to choosing the title.					
2.	I contributed to making the plot (story).					
3.	I contributed to writing the first draft.					
4.	I contributed to writing the second draft.					
5.	I rehearsed my part by myself.					
6.	I rehearsed the drama with my group members.					
7.	Our drama took a reasonable amount of time.					
8.	Our drama was interesting.					
9.	I contributed equally to the performance.					
10.	I used expressive body language.					
11.	I was confident and cheerful.					
12.	I helped to make the props and audio/visual effects.					
	Total = _____ /60					

My comments:

By yourself

- Review what you have done in this Unit and prepare for the next Unit.

REVIEW: Browse the website for Unit 9.

PREVIEW: Browse the website for Unit 10.

PREPARE: Look at the activities in Unit 10.

ORGANIZE: Cut out this page and put it in the portfolio pocket.

Unit 10 Print Media Project

Here are some imaginary headlines from the future. Do you think they will come true?

Pairs

- Mark your opinion from 1 to 4.
- 1 = No way. 2 = Very unlikely. 3 = Possible. 4 = Very likely.
- Talk about the headlines together.

Global News

Wednesday, December 21, 2112

HOTEL OPENS ON THE MOON

Cure for cancer discovered

World peace declared

Scientist travels back in time

No snow or ice in Antarctica

Robots Teach English

New planes use solar energy

Oldest woman in the world 150 years old today

Tigers extinct

ASIAN-AMERICAN WOMAN PRESIDENT GIVES STATE OF THE UNION SPEECH

*In this Unit, your group will make a newspaper or magazine (writing) and present it (speaking).

Campus Friends: Reporters

Track 22

The six friends have become reporters on the school English newspaper. Chang-min, Kadi, and Deniz are working on their articles together. Can you work out who is speaking?

Groups

- Look at the dialog on this page together.
- Write the names of the speakers in the column on the left.
- Perform the dialog together.
- Check unfamiliar words in the Glossary (▶pages 147-154).

	Good morning, you two. What are you doing?
	Hello, Chang-min. Kadi and I are working on our articles.
	Isn't it great? We've all become reporters?
	Sure. What are you writing about?
	I'm doing an article about Turkey.
	And I'm writing about oriental medicine. How about you?
	I might write about the Photography Club.
	That's a good idea. I have some photos of Turkey, as well.
	I hope my oriental medicine article is good enough.
	I'm sure it will be.
	Have you made an outline?
	Yes, I have. I'm making my first draft now.
	Show it to us when you finish and we'll edit it.
	Don't forget to have some interesting photos!

*The complete dialog is in the **Answer Section**, at the back of the book.

Reading: Print Media

Track 23

Groups

In this Unit, we look at newspapers, newsletters, magazines, and brochures. Your project will be one of these types of print media. Read these articles together and talk about them.

Print Media Newsletter

December 2014
Volume 1, Issue 1

Freshman English, (123) 456-7890

Highlights

First printing press	2
History of print	3
Paper making	4
Recycling newspapers	5
Print media online	6
Editorial	7
Opinion	8

Brochures

These give information to visitors to museums, national parks, tourist sites, etc. They contain information about the sites and photos of the landmarks.

Another type of brochure is used for concerts and other entertainment. The concert brochure contains information about the performers, the music, the conductor, and the composer.

A stage-play brochure contains information about the play, the actors, the director, and the writer.

Newspapers

When we think of print media we usually think of newspapers.

The first modern-style newspaper was published in Germany in 1605. Early newspapers were often closed down by rulers who didn't want to be criticized. *The Public Occurrences* (1690) was published for one day only in the US.

In London, the first newspaper was the *Daily Courant* (1702). In 1784, the *Daily Universal Register* began. This was soon renamed *The Times* and became one of the major world newspapers. *The Pennsylvania Evening Post* (1783) was also renamed and is now *The New York Times*, another world-leader.

There are about 1,500 daily newspapers in the world, and they are read by 130 million people. However, only 30% of young people read newspapers, compared with 60% thirty years ago. Electronic media is making life difficult for traditional newspapers and many of them can now be read online.

Magazines

Whenever we go to the doctor, dentist, hair stylist, or even coffee shop, there are usually magazines for us to read. Like newspapers, they give information on many topics. However, they are more colorful, with lots of images and adverts.

The word 'magazine' originally referred to a place where grain or dynamite was stored. Because of this, Edward Cave started his *Gentleman's Magazine* (1731) as a storehouse of information. It was very popular and others soon appeared in the UK and the US.

There are two main types of magazine. The first type concentrates on news and current affairs (*Newsweek*, *Time*, *The Field*, *The Spectator*, etc.). The second type aims at certain types of people: women, teens, brides, golfers, fishers, bikers, etc. Because certain types of people read these magazines, they often contain lots of adverts. Marketers know that the people who are likely to buy their products are reading their adverts.

Newsletters

Newsletters give special information to a small group of people. They are often made by clubs, associations, companies, and societies, for example, a church newsletter, or a university alumni newsletter.

Print Media Project: Preparation

Your group will make a print-media project. You will make a newspaper/magazine/newsletter/brochure together and present it to the other groups.

Groups

1. Your print media should be attractive, informative, and interesting.
2. Each member of the group should write at least one article.
3. You can include photos, games, puzzles, etc.
4. Each person will introduce part of the project during the presentation.
5. This is your final assignment, so do your best, and enjoy the project!

Step 1: Choose your print media. Here are some suggestions:

Art Magazine	School Newspaper	Travel Brochure
Cooking Magazine	(Your Major) Newspaper	Concert Brochure
Culture Magazine	Club Newsletter	Exhibition Brochure
Fashion Magazine	(Your Major) Newsletter	Museum Brochure
Health Magazine	Society Newsletter	Performance Brochure
Sports Magazine	School Alumni Newsletter	Business Brochure

Step 2: Discuss the content of your print media. Here are some suggestions:

Agony aunt	Editorial	Horoscopes	Reviews
Business section	Fashion page	Local news	Sports page
Cartoon strips	Feature article	Political news	Travel page
Cooking page	Financial page	Puzzles	Weather forecast
Culture page	Health page	Readers' letters	World news

Step 3: Discuss your roles. What will each person do? (Brainstorming)

Print Media: Planning

Now that you have decided on the type and content of your print media, the next step is planning. Use this page to help you make a plan of your print media. Write the names of articles, writers, etc., in the boxes.

Groups

- Decide how many pages you will have.
- Decide what will go on each page.
- Decide who will write the articles for each page.
- Decide who will make the graphics and design the layout.

Page 1	Page 2	Page 3
Page 4	Page 5	Page 6
Page 7	Page 8	Page 9
Page 10	Page 11	Page 12

Brainstorming: My Article(s)

By yourself What will your main article be about? Use this page to brainstorm and outline your first draft. If there is time, why not write two articles? (▶ pages 105 and 106)

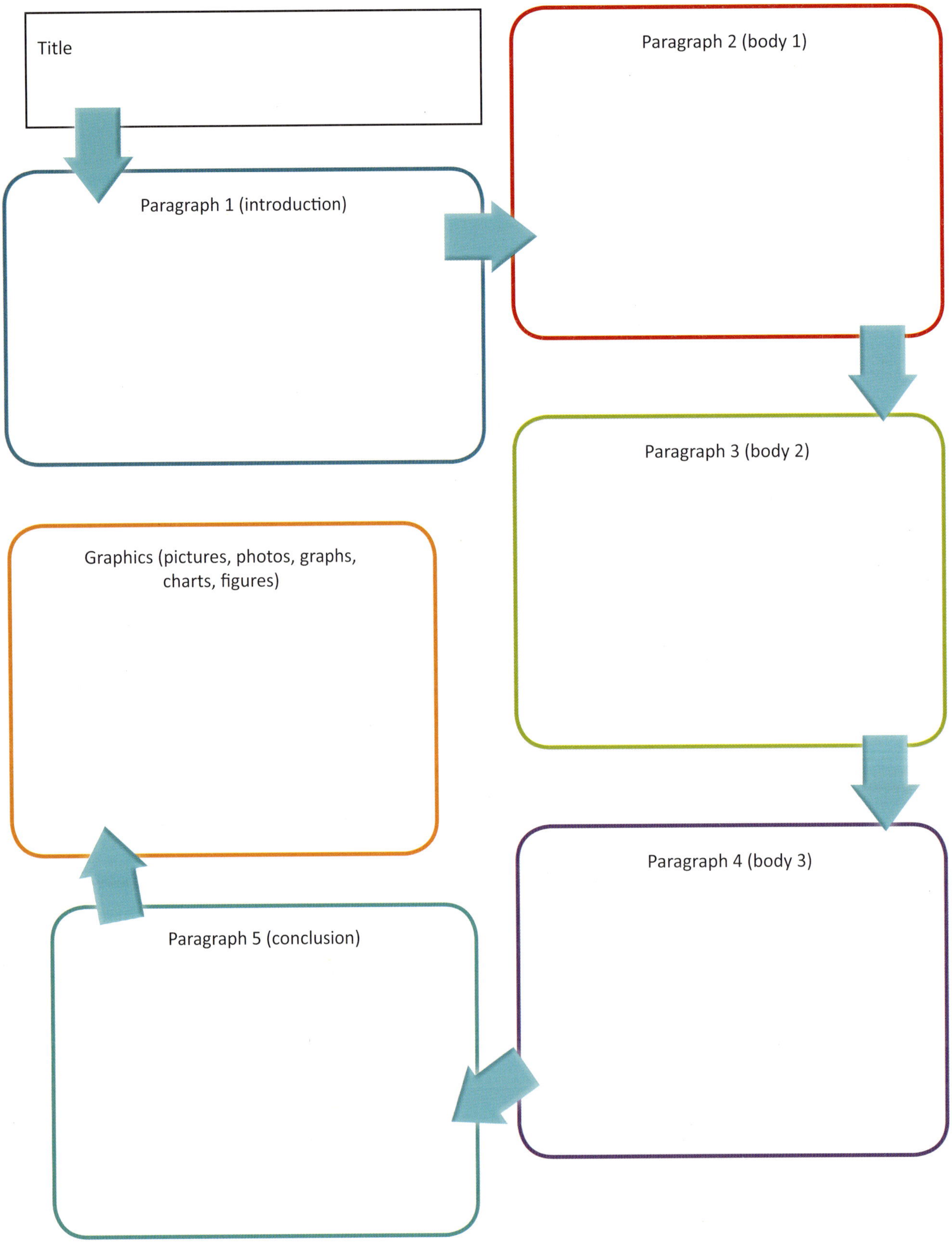

My First Article: First Draft

By yourself

Write the first draft of your first article here. If you use a computer, print the file and stick it on this page. Don't forget the images!

Pairs

- Ask a classmate to look at your article.
- Edit the article together.

My First Article: Final Draft

By yourself

Write the final draft of your first article here based on the peer editing (▶page 103). If you use a computer, print the file and stick it on this page. Don't forget the images!

My Second Article: **First Draft**

By yourself

If you have time, you can write a different article now. Write your first draft here. If you use a computer, print the file and stick it on this page. Don't forget the images!

Pairs

- Ask a classmate to look at your article.
- Edit the article together.

My Second Article: **Final Draft**

By yourself Write the final draft of your second article here based on the peer editing (▶page 105). If you use a computer, print the file and stick it on this page. Don't forget the images!

Presentation Checklist

It is time to make the final version of the print media and give a presentation about it.

Groups

1. Collect all the articles written by group members.
2. Make your final print media project and print it out.
    - You will show this to other students in your presentation.
3. Look at the checklist below and prepare for your presentation.

Presentation Checklist

			✓
Planning	Brainstorm ideas for the presentation.	Groups	
	Make a plan for your presentation.		
	Decide what each person will do.		
	Decide how long each person will speak.		
Preparing	Prepare your presentation materials.	By yourself	
	Write your speech.		
Practicing	Rehearse your part of the presentation.		
	Practice in front of a mirror. Look at your body language.		
	Ask a friend to watch you and give you advice.		
	Record your voice and listen to it.		
	Remember your speech.		
	Practice speaking clearly and slowly.		
Pre-presenting	Check the presentation room.	Groups	
	Check the seating layout (audience).		
	Check the lighting and equipment.		
Presenting	Wear smart clothes. Make a good impression.	Everyone	
	Begin and end on time.		
	Give out handouts before you start.		
	Use note cards. Don't read your speech.		
	Use positive body language. Smile.		
	Make eye contact with the audience.		
Assessment	Assess your own performance (▶ page 108).		
	Assess the other groups' performances (▶ page 109).		

Project and Presentation: Self-assessment

By yourself How was your project? How was your presentation? Were you satisfied? Check (✓) the percentage that matches your efforts and achievements.

The project	25%	50%	75%	100%
1. I helped in the decision and planning stage (▶pages 100-101).				
2. I wrote my own article(s) (▶pages 102-106).				
3. I peer-edited articles of my group members (▶pages 103, 105).				
4. I spoke in English with my group members.				
5. I helped to make the final version of the print media.				

The presentation	25%	50%	75%	100%
6. I prepared for the presentation diligently (▶page 107).				
7. I wore suitable clothes (▶page 107).				
8. I spoke for the correct time.				
9. I spoke clearly, without hesitation.				
10. I remembered my speech.				
11. I was confident and cheerful.				
12. I made eye contact with the audience.				
13. I used positive body language.				
14. I enjoyed giving the presentation.				

My comments

Project and Presentation: Peer-assessment

By yourself How were the other projects? Write the numbers that match your opinion.

4 = Yes, definitely; **3** = Yes, OK; **2** = Not really; **1** = No, not at all.

1. General (Presentation)	Gp 1	Gp 2	Gp 3	Gp 4	Gp 5
Was the presentation well prepared?					
Did it have a clear structure (beginning, middle, end)?					
Was the presentation interesting and informative?					
Was the timing well managed?					

2. Project (Print Media)	Gp 1	Gp 2	Gp 3	Gp 4	Gp 5
Was the project well made?					
Was the project interesting and creative?					
Did the presenters explain their project clearly?					
Did every presenter explain a part of the project?					

3. Delivery (Verbal Communication)	Gp 1	Gp 2	Gp 3	Gp 4	Gp 5
Did the presenters speak clearly?					
Did they remember their speeches?					
Did they speak without hesitation?					

4. Body Language (Non-verbal Communication)	Gp 1	Gp 2	Gp 3	Gp 4	Gp 5
Did the presenters use positive body language?					
Did they make eye contact with the audience?					
Were they confident? Did they smile?					

5. Overall Impression (including Q&A)	Gp 1	Gp 2	Gp 3	Gp 4	Gp 5
Did the presenters dress suitably?					
Did they answer questions well?					
Total Score (maximum = 64)					

Group 1: comments	
Group 2: comments	
Group 3: comments	
Group 4: comments	
Group 5: comments	

Final Discussion: Looking Back and Looking Ahead

Pairs

- We are at the end of the course.
- How do you feel about your English now?
- Talk about these questions together.

How was your freshman year in university?
- What is the most important thing you have learned this year?

What did you learn this semester?
- How are your English skills now?
- Did your English skills improve?

Will you continue to learn English?
- Yes: How will you do this?
- No: Why not?

What are your plans for the next few years?
- Do you want to be an exchange student?
- Do you want to be an intern?
- Do you want to do graduate studies?

What are your plans for the future?
- What are your career plans?
- What are your personal plans?

What are the most important things in your life?
- Health? Love? Family? Friends?
- Wealth? Power? Money? A good job?

Review Page: Freshman English 2

How was the course? Did it help you learn the English you need for university and for your future? How about you? Did you do your best? Did you have a positive attitude?

By yourself

- Think deeply about the questions on this page.
- Fill in your answers.

1) What was the most impressive thing in this course?

2) How was the teacher?

3) How were your assignments?

4) How were your self-assessments?

5) How were your projects?

6) How were your presentations?

7) How was your participation?

8) How was your attitude?

9) How are your speaking skills now?

10) How are your writing skills now?

11) How are your confidence and motivation now?

12) What do you need to improve?

By yourself

- Turn back to page 20 and try the self-assessment again.
- What is your score this time? How much have you improved?

AU REVOIR!

Now it's time to say goodbye to everyone.
Did you make any friends on the course?
Is there anything you want to say to them?

Tot ziens

Hasta la Vista

Adios

さようなら

Ciao

Adieu

Tot wederom

Nägemist

GOODBYE

Auf Wiedersehen

Hoşçakal

안녕!

再見

Word Bank

These resources will help you improve your spoken and written English. Refer to them regularly and use the words and phrases whenever you can.

Contents

	pages
Adjectives: Feelings and Emotions, Positive Qualities	114
Transitions, Discussion Words, and Conversation Gambits	115
Marking code	122
Unit 2: Chang-min, short bio	123
Unit 2: Ji-won, Minghua, short bios	124
Unit 2: Deniz, Kadi, short bios	125
Unit 3: Giving Advice	126
Unit 3: Résumé 1, Kadi Saar	127
Unit 3: Résumé 2, Deniz Osman	128
Unit 3: Résumé 3, Lee Chang-min	129
Unit 3: University Schools and Departments, Job Departments and Office Positions	130
Unit 5: Interview Q & As	131
Unit 5: Three Types of Verbs	134
Unit 6: Campus Friends: Traveling	135
Unit 6: Campus Friends: Healing the World	136
Unit 6: Personal Statement: Kadi Saar	137
Unit 7: Senior Advice to Freshmen	138
Unit 7: Relative Clauses	139
Unit 7: Email Cover Letter	140
Unit 7: Story-based Cover Letter: Emily Stounton	141
Unit 9: Extra Role-plays	142
Unit 9: Finish the Story	145
Work-related Proverbs	146
Glossary of Key Words	147
Answer Section	155
Plan of Writing Process and Assignments	162

Adjectives: Feelings and Emotions

adorable
affectionate
afraid
alive
ambitious
angry
annoyed
anxious
ashamed
awkward
bad
beautiful
blue
bold
bored
brave
calm
capable
cautious
childish
clumsy
comfortable
compassionate
competitive
confident
confused
content
curious
daring
delighted
depressed
determined
disappointed
discouraged
doubtful
eager
embarrassed
emotional
energetic
enthusiastic
envious
excited
fantastic
fearless
foolish
fortunate
free
friendly
frightened
frustrated
glad
good
grateful
great
greedy
guilty
happy
hateful
helpless
homesick
honored
hopeful
horrible
humble
impatient
important
inspired
intelligent
interested
involved
jealous
jolly
joyful
lazy
lonely
lost
loved
loving
marvelous
miserable
naughty
negative
nervous
optimistic
overjoyed
overworked
passive
peaceful
pessimistic
pleased
powerful
proud
puzzled
quiet
regretful
relaxed
relieved
ridiculous
rude
sad
safe
satisfied
scared
selfish
sensitive
sentimental
serious
shy
sick
sleepy
smart
so-so
special
strong
stubborn
stupid
surprised
suspicious
sympathetic
tense
terrible
terrific
thankful
tired
uncomfortable
uneasy
unhappy
warm
wise
wonderful
worried

Adjectives: Positive Qualities

active
affectionate
amusing
artistic
aware
capable
careful
caring
cheerful
clever
comical
competent
confident
considerate
cooperative
courageous
courteous
creative
dependable
devoted
earnest
easygoing
efficient
energetic
enthusiastic
forgiving
friendly
funny
generous
gentle
good-hearted
good-humored
good-natured
happy
hard-working
helpful
heroic
honest
honorable
humble
humorous
idealistic
imaginative
independent
intelligent
interesting
inventive
joyous
keen
kind
kind-hearted
lighthearted
lively
logical
lovable
loving
loyal
mature
merciful
natural
objective
open-minded
organized
original
outgoing
patient
playful
pleasant
polite
practical
rational
reasonable
reflective
reliable
resourceful
respectful
responsible
sensible
sensitive
sincere
skillful
sociable
sympathetic
tender
thorough
thoughtful
trustworthy
truthful
understanding
unique
unselfish
warm
warm-hearted
wise
witty

Transitions, Discussion Words, and Conversation Gambits

The words and phrases in this section can be used in the speaking and writing activities in this book. The informal expressions (in blue) are not used in formal writing.

Adding a point | 내용 추가할 때

First,
Second,
Next,
Also,
Again,

Besides,
Moreover,
In addition,
Likewise,
Similarly,
Otherwise,

What's more,
Furthermore,
As well as …
On top of that,
For example,
For instance,

Equally important,
In the same way,
Not only … but also
Not only that but …
Plus the fact that …
Not to mention that …

Oh I almost forgot …
And another thing
Just a small point
That reminds me …

Advantages and disadvantages | 장단점 표현할 때

On the one hand,
On the other hand,
One advantage is that …
One disadvantage is that …
The positive side of it is that …
The negative aspect of it is that …

The problem is …
One drawback is that …
Another thing is that …
I'm afraid to say that …
The main advantage is that …
The main disadvantage is that …

Advice | 조언할 때

Have you thought about … ?
I advise you to …
I think you ought to …
I think you should …
I think you'd better …
If I were in your place, I'd …
If I were in your position, I'd ....

If I were in your shoes, I'd …
If I were you, I'd …
It is advisable to …
One way would be to …
Perhaps you could …
The best thing for you to do is …

What about …ing?
Why don't you … ?
Why not … ?
You'd better …
You could always …
Your best bet is to …

Advice after the event | 어떤 일이 발생한 후 조언할 때

What you should have done was….
You shouldn't have …
You should have …
I wouldn't have done that.

Why didn't you……?
If I had been you, I would have….
You really should have asked me.

Agreement and disagreement | 찬성과 반대 표현할 때

True. Yes.
I agree. I disagree.
I don't agree.
That's right.
That's true.
That's very true.
Yes, of course.
I agree with you that ...
I know what you mean.
You are absolutely right.

Agreed.
Me too! So do I.
OK. Right.
I couldn't agree more.
I agree with you there.
You are absolutely right.
That's what I thought.
I'll go along with that.
That's what I thought.

I can't agree.
Absolutely not.
Of course not.
That's not possible.
You can't be serious.
I think you are mistaken.
We'll have to agree to differ.
Yes, but don't you think ...?
Yes, but on the other hand ...

Approval and disapproval | 승인/찬성과 반대의견 표현할 때

Excellent.
Very good.
Well done.
I approve of ...
I disapprove of ...
I don't enjoy ...

I love it.
It's great!
Marvelous.
Wonderful!
Fantastic!
I'll give it 10.
I think it's fantastic.

It's my cup of tea.
It's out of this world.
It's not for me.
It's not my cup of tea.
It doesn't turn me on.
It doesn't do anything for me.
I'm afraid I disapprove of ...

Argument and counter argument | 주장과 반론을 제기할 때

The first thing to point out is ...
Let's look at the facts.
One argument in support of...
The second reason for...
It is a well-known fact that...
It is often said that...
On the other hand ...

Anyway,
OK, but ...
Yes, but ...
Even so,
Possibly, but ...
That's true, but ...
But don't forget ...

But what about ...
Even if that is so,
Look at it this way.
That may be so, but ...
Yes, but don't forget ...
You have a point, but ...
That's probably true, but ...

Asking for clarification | 설명 요청

Can you explain ... ?
Can you say that again?
Do you mean to say ... ?
Does this mean ...?
How come ...?
What did you say?
What do you mean by ...?
Why do you say that?

Asking for opinions | 의견 물을 때

How about you?
What do you think?
What would you say?
Do you have an opinion?
What do you think of ...?
Do you agree with the others?
What's your opinion of/about ...?
Would you like to tell us your opinion?

Asking for repetition | 한번 더 말해 달라고 요청할 때

What did you say?
What was that again?
One more time, please.
Could you repeat that?
I'm sorry, I didn't hear you.
Could you say that again, please?
Would you mind repeating that?

Breaking in | 상대방 말 중단할 때

Excuse me. Sorry, but …
Can I come in here?
Can I add something?
Can I say something here?
I'd like to comment on that.
Excuse me for interrupting, but …
I don't want to interrupt, but …
May I interrupt for a moment?

Cause and effect | 원인과 결과 표현할 때

So,
Thus,
Hence,
Then …

Due to …
Since …
So that …
Because …

Therefore,
Wherefore
Accordingly,
As a result,

Otherwise,
Thereupon
Consequently,
Subsequently,

For this reason,
For these reasons,
For this purpose,
With the result that …

Certainty and uncertainty | 확신과 불확신 표현할 때

Certainly. Absolutely.
Of course.
No doubt.
Without a doubt.
There is no doubt that ...
The problem is …

I'm convinced that …
I'm (am) certain that ...
I am sure that ...
Yes, but …
I'm not sure.
Possibly, but …

I don't see how …
I doubt whether …
Yes, but don't forget …
I'm pretty sure that…
Yes, but the problem is …
What I'm worried about is …

Changing the subject | 화제 전환

Speaking of …
By the way,
That reminds me …
Oh, before I forget, …
I'm sorry to change the subject, but …
It's funny you should say that, but …

Checking comprehension | 이해 체크

OK?
OK so far?
Do you see?
Are you with me?
Is that clear?
Have you got it?

Do you follow?
Do you understand?
Does it make sense?
Shall I say it again?
Are you still with me?

Clarifying | 설명/해명/부연할 때

Let me explain.
Let me put it this way.
Let me put it another way.
To put it more clearly,
For example,

I said … What I said was …
I mean … What I mean to say is…
What I meant was …
What I'm saying is …
What I'm trying to say is ...

Compare and contrast | 비교와 대조 표현할 때

As (adj) as …	Larger than …	Or … But …	In contrast,
As though …	Smaller than …	Yet … Still,	Rather than …
Likewise,	More (adj) than …	In fact,	Even when …
Similar to …	More than …	Rather,	Even though …
Similarly,	Greater than …	Unlike …,	Nevertheless,
Better than …	Less than …	Instead,	On the contrary,
Worse than …	At the same time,	Whereas …	On the one hand,
Bigger than …	By comparison,	However,	On the other hand,

Comprehension and incomprehension | 이해 여부 표현할 때

Yes. I see.	OK. Right. I get it.
I understand.	Pardon?
I'm with you.	I don't get it.
Now I follow you.	You've lost me.
I see what you mean.	Sorry, you've lost me.
Now I understand.	Sorry, I don't follow you.
I don't understand.	Sorry, I didn't catch the last part.
I'm not with you.	I didn't understand a word you said.

Concession | 상대의 말에도 일리가 있고 옳다고 인정할 때

Of course.	All right.
You have a point there.	OK.
That's a good point.	If you say so.
I take your point.	Yes, that's true.
While that may be true,	You've got a point.
I can't argue with that.	That's true, but …

Deduction and reasoning | 연역에 의한 결론 및 추론

If…, then …	…, so it must be …	We can conclude that …
Therefore, …	This indicates that …	These arguments show that …
This means that …	This proves that …	These arguments suggest that …
It follows that …	This shows that …	This points to the conclusion that …

Direction | 방향을 표현할 때

here	nearly	across from	to the left	above	not far from here
there	opposite	far from	to the right	below	just down the street
beyond	next to	over there	straight ahead	under	You can't miss it.

Disappointment | 실망/유감 표현

Oh, no!
Oh, dear!
What a pity!
That's a pity.
What a shame!
It's a shame!
That's so sad.
How disappointing!
I feel (really) let down.
I feel really disappointed.
I don't know what to say.

Displeasure | 불쾌/불만 표현

I don't like it.
It's horrible/terrible!
I can't stand it.
I don't like to think of it.
It makes me sad/unhappy.
I can't tell you how sad/angry I am.

Emphasis | 강조할 때

Again, Also, Truly, Really, Surely, Chiefly, Besides, Certainly, In fact, In truth, Indeed, Above all, Of course, Especially, In addition, Particularly, Furthermore,

Expressing surprise | 놀람을 표시할 때

Are you sure?
That is amazing!
I can't believe it!
I am surprised!
I'm shocked!
That's extraordinary!
I'm surprised to hear that!
Oh? What?
Oh, really?
My goodness!
Good Heavens!
Are you joking?
You're pulling my leg!
That's one for the books!

Generalizing | 일반화시켜 표현할 때

Usually, As a rule, Generally, In general, Normally, Ordinarily, By and large, On the whole, In most cases, For the most part, In my experience, Generally speaking, More often than not,

Getting started | 시작할 때

Let's begin.
Shall I start?
Shall we begin?
How can we begin?
Let's get started.
Let's get the ball rolling.
Who would like to start?
Would someone like to kick things off?
Does anyone have something to say?

Giving an opinion | 자신의 의사/견해를 표현할 때

I think …
In my view,
As I see it, ...
My view is ...
To my mind,
I think (that) …
I suppose …
I suspect that …
In my opinion,
I believe that …
Well, personally,
I personally think …
It's my opinion that …
From my point of view,
Not everyone will agree with me, but …

Giving reasons | 방향을 표현할 때

First of all, …
Secondly, …
That's why …
Because …

For this reason, …
Besides that,
Because of that, …
The reason why …

The main reason is …
The main thing is …
On the one hand, …
On the other hand, …

The other reason is …
Another reason is …
And on top of that,
And finally,

Illustrating | 예시할 때

In this case,
For example,
As an example,
For instance,
For one thing,
For another thing,
As an illustration,

Making a point | 주장을 강조할 때

The point is …
My point is …
What I mean is …
What I want to say is …
We must remember that …
We have to remember that ...
We should not forget that ...

The point I'm trying to make is …
Let's not forget that …

Pleasure | 즐거움/기쁨/만족 표현할 때

It's very pleasing.
It makes me feel good.
I am really delighted.
I cannot tell you how happy I am.
It gives me great pleasure.

Wonderful!
Fantastic!
I feel great.

How marvelous!
I'm really pleased.
I'm over the moon.

Predicting | 예측/예견

If …,
If I ever …
When …
Whenever …
As soon as …
By the time …
Unless …

Preference | 선호도 표현할 때

I prefer to …
I like to …
I love … ing
I would like to …
I really like to …
I would prefer to …
My preference is …

What do you prefer?
What do you like most?
I like apples more than bananas.
I prefer apples to bananas.
My favorite is ….
I'd rather have a cup of coffee.

Requesting | 요청할 때

Can I ask a question?
May I ask something?
Do you know … ?
I'd like to know …
I'm interested in …
Could you tell me …?
Do you mind if I ask a question?

Returning to the topic | 화제로 되돌아올 때

Anyway, …
In any case, …
As I was saying, …
Getting back to the topic, …
Where was I?
What was I saying?
To get back to what I was saying, …

Sequencing | 순서대로 나열하거나 시간 순서 표현할 때

Next,	For now,	At first,	In conclusion,	Since then,
Then,	In time,	First of all,	To begin with,	The next step is …
Soon,	In turn,	After that,	In the first place,	In the meantime,
Earlier,	Later on,	Meanwhile,	At the same time,	Simultaneously,
Later,	Finally,	Afterwards,	For the time being,	With this in mind,

Stating the issue | 문제를 제시하거나 진술할 때

The trouble is …	The point is …	The thing is …	The real question is …
The problem is …	The real problem is …	Don't forget that …	

Suggesting | 제안할 때

Let's ... Why not … ?
I suggest ...
I've an idea.
How about … ?
Why don't you … ?
You can always ...
Do you feel like ...?
Have you ever thought of ...?

Surprising facts | 놀라운 사실 전할 때

Surprisingly,
Oddly enough,
Strangely enough,
Do you realize that …?
Believe it or not,
The surprising thing is …
It may sound strange, but …
You may not believe it, but …

Summarizing | 요약하거나 결론을 도출할 때

Briefly,	In short,	In any case,	On the whole,	In the long run,
In brief,	Finally,	In any event,	In summary,	All things considered,
After all,	By and large,	To sum up,	To summarize,	As I have shown,
All in all,	On balance,	In conclusion,	Therefore,	

Synthesis | 논리적으로 종합할 때

Actually,	To be honest,	We can safely say that ...
Frankly,	It's fair to say that …	The truth of the matter is …
On balance,	In the final analysis, ...	The fact of the matter is that…
On reflection,	To tell you the truth,	

Wants, needs, and wishes | 필요/요구/희망사항 표현할 때

I want to …	I prefer ...	I fancy ...	I wouldn't say no to …
I need to …	I would like to …	If only …	I wouldn't mind ...
I wish …	I am quite anxious to ...	I feel like ...	Wouldn't it be nice if …?

Marking Code

Code	Problem	Example
C	Capitalization	C C C C C my name is gary. i come from the isle of man.
P	Punctuation	P P P P P I like music. movies: and hiking? How, about you! , , . ?
Gr1	Apostrophes Personal pronouns	Gr1 Gr1 Gr1 Thats not mine dog. Im certain about that. That's my I'm
Gr2	Singular/plural Count/non-count	Gr2 Gr2 Gr2 Gr2 Nobody have eaten many meats or fruits. has much meat fruit
Sp	Spelling	Sp Sp Sp Sp The trainn doesn't arive at the staytion untill 5 pm. train arrive station until
Pr	Prepositions	Pr Pr Pr Put the square in top about the circle and next the cube. on of next to
Art	Articles	Art Art Art ~~The~~ Hallasan is ^ highest mountain in ~~the~~ South Korea. the
S/v	Subject/verb agreement	S/v A large percentage of the population are watching the World Cup. is
WO	Word order	WO My [sport] [favorite] is fencing.

✓ Paragraph Checklist

- ☐ Title
- ☐ Topic sentence
- ☐ Concluding sentence
- ☐ Unity (only one idea)
- ☐ Cohesion 1 (smooth flow of ideas)
- ☐ Cohesion 2 (pronouns, articles, transitions)
- ☐ Continuity (each sentence leads into the next)

Writing a Short Bio: Sample 2 Unit 2, page 17

Track 24

This is the bio of Lee Chang-min. It is the second sample bio. The first sample is on page 17.

Biodata of Lee Chang-min
Palgong APT
Daegu, Republic of Korea

Lee Chang-min graduated from Apsan High School, where he was the editor of the school's Korean newspaper and class representative. He is a part-time tutor of Math and a keen tennis player. He was on the team that came second in the high school tennis championship last year. Chang-min is a member of the university photography club and has a certificate in computer skills. He has traveled around Korea and hopes to travel around the world in the future. He wants to study Earth Sciences so that he can become an eco-scientist and develop renewable energy and green technology. (100 words)

Education:	Apsan High School. Editor of school newspaper, class representative
Jobs:	Math tutor (part-time)
Interests:	Tennis
Clubs:	University Photography Club
Skills:	Computer certificate
Travel:	Inside Korea
Prizes:	School tennis team, regional championship
Future:	Eco-scientist, green technology

Writing a Short Bio: Samples 3 and 4 Unit 2, page 17

Track 25

Here are the bios of Moon Ji-won and Zhang Minghua.

Biodata of Moon Ji-won
Moojigae APT
Gyeongju, South Korea

Moon Ji-won went to Gyeongju High School, where she was president of the English Conversation Club. She has studied English in a summer school in Indonesia, and received a prize for perfect attendance. Ji-won has taught Korean to foreigners for one semester and she also volunteers in an orphanage. Ms. Moon likes swimming in her spare time and is a member of the University Guitar Club. She wants to study nutrition and has a cooking certificate from a private institute. After being an exchange student in Europe, she hopes to be a food consultant and work for the government. (99 words)

Biodata of Zhang Minghua
112 Heping Lu
Lantian, People's Republic of China

Zhang Minghua went to Lantian High School near Xi'an, China, where he was president of the *TIME* reading group. He helped his father in his export company before coming to Korea to study International Trade. Minghua enjoys playing basketball and has traveled all around China with his school team, winning many prizes. He goes to the health club every day and hopes to get on the university basketball team. Mr. Zhang wants to improve his English and Korean and is also studying Japanese. He intends to do an MBA in the USA before returning to China to run his own company. (101 words)

Writing a Short Bio: Samples 5 and 6 Unit 2, page 17

Track 26

Here are the bios of Deniz Osman and Kadi Saar.

Biodata of Deniz Osman
Timur Heights, Kat 5 Apt. 3
Ankara, Republic of Turkey

Deniz Osman came to Korea to study engineering. He was president of the Chess Club in Ankara High School and played on the school soccer team. He was a volunteer at a number of engineering fairs in Ankara and has travelled around Europe during his vacations. Deniz goes mountain biking in his spare time and is also a keen astronomer. He likes to observe the night sky whenever he has a chance. Mr. Osman hopes to be an exchange student in the USA in his Junior year, before returning to Turkey as a geotechnical engineer and working on major development projects. (101 words)

Biodata of Kadi Saar
Paldoski Str 7
10345 Tallinn, Republic of Estonia

Kadi Saar went to the Tallinn Gymnasium, where she was a member of the English Drama Club. She played the part of Cordelia in Shakespeare's *King Lear*. Kadi worked part-time in a pharmacy before coming to Korea to study Oriental Medicine. She likes learning languages and playing the violin. She has a certificate in First Aid and often helps the medics at sporting events. Ms. Saar is very interested in acupuncture, pressure points, and herbal medicine. She is learning Chinese characters in order to study Oriental Medicine in Korea and then return to Estonia and set up her own clinic. (100 words)

Giving Advice: Situations Unit 3, page 22

Here are some more situations to add to those on page 22. What advice would you give to these people?

I don't know what major to choose or what to do when I graduate. What shall I do?

Clueless

I am so busy. I don't have time for any exercise. What shall I do?

Gym

I want to travel this vacation but I don't have any money. What shall I do?

Rambler

My laptop crashed and I lost all my files. What shall I do?

Antivirus

I had a great time studying English in Australia and I flew back from Brisbane today. However, my luggage is still in Brisbane. What shall I do?

Worried

I went to the doctor today. She told me to go on a diet. I love eating. What shall I do?

Gourmet

I really want to give up smoking. I have tried many times, but I just can't stop. What shall I do?

Smoky Joe

I keep oversleeping and being late to class. What shall I do?

Sleepyhead

I can't get to sleep these days. I keep worrying about my grades. What shall I do?

Sleepless in Daegu

My roommate is untidy and dirty. I think hygiene is very important. What shall I do?

Dusty

I saw my boyfriend with my best friend. They were holding hands. What shall I do?

Angry

I saw my friend cheating on the exam. He told me not to say anything. What shall I do?

Puzzled

Sample Résumé (1) Unit 3, page 25

Kadi Saar

59 Paldoski Street, Tallinn, 10345, Republic of Estonia
T: +372 123-4567 F: +372 123-5678 E: ksaar@estmail.net

Objective

To become an expert in Oriental Medicine (acupuncture, pressure points, and herbal medicine), in order to set up a clinic in Estonia.

Experience

Pharmacy assistant (Part-time) July 2010 – Dec 2011
Duties included maintaining the storage and security of the drugs, entering patient information into the computer database, preparing compound drugs, answering the telephone, serving customers, and ordering drugs from suppliers.

First Aid Volunteer Apr 2008 – Aug 2011
Helped medics at sporting events in Tallinn. Basic first aid for sports injuries.

Education

Kyungpook National University Mar 2012 – present
School of Pharmacy. Expected date of graduation August 2016.

Tallinn Gymnasium Sept 2007 – June 2010
Graduated with honors. Member of the English Drama Club. Played Cordelia in Shakespeare's *King Lear*.

Skills

Computer literate in various applications, including MS Office, Open Office, Pharmacy software, HTML, CSS.

First Aid certificate, Estonian Red Cross

Estonian and English languages (fluent); Korean (Basic)

Chinese Calligraphy (Basic)

Violin: Estonian Academy of Music, Grade 5

Interests

Music, Oriental philosophy and culture, Languages

Sample Résumé (2) Unit 3, page 25

Deniz Osman

Timur Heights, Kat 5 Apt. 3 • Ankara • Republic of Turkey 06470
• Phone: +90 312-987-6543 • E-Mail: Osman59@tarkis.net

Objective

I would like to contribute to Turkish society by becoming an expert geotechnical engineer and working on major development projects such as roads, dams, and bridges in my home country.

Experience

Volunteer, engineering fairs 2010 - 2012

- Working with admin staff in the exhibition site
- Contacting exhibiting companies
- Helping to set up the booths
- Guiding visitors around the fairs and helping them

Education

Kyungpook National University 2013 - now
Engineering, Earth Sciences, B.Sc. Expected date of graduation August 2016

Ankara High School 2008 - 2012
High School Finishing Examinations (passed)
President, Chess Club; School soccer team

Skills

Languages: Turkish, Arabic (advanced), English (Intermediate), Korean (Basic)
Computer: Engineering software, MS Office, Photoshop, Video software, XHTML

Interests

Astronomy, mountain biking, traveling

Reference

Dr. Mohamed Demir, mdemir@kurdish.org

Sample Résumé (3) Unit 3, page 25

Lee Chang-min

Palgong APT 201-302, Daegu 738-682
Phone: 053-987-5559 • HP: 018-929-0303 • E-Mail: cmlee@email.net

Career objectives

I intend to study earth sciences at graduate level so that I can become an expert eco-scientist and develop renewable energy and green technology.

Education

B.Sc. (Expected 2016) Earth Sciences, Kyungpook National University

Apsan High School (2009 – 2012) Editor of the school newspaper, class representative, member of the school team that came 2nd in the high school tennis championship

Experience

- Private lessons in Math to high school students 2012 - present

Skills and Awards

- Computer skills, KCA Certificate, Grade 3
- Tennis, Finalist in the East Daegu Youth Cup, 2012
- Newspaper editing and formatting
- Korean and English (fluent)

Interests

- Tennis, Photography, Travel

References

Prof. Ryu Son-gil
Department of Earth Sciences
Kyungpook National University
80 Daehak-ro, Buk-gu, Daegu 702-701
Tel: 02-345-6789

Mr. Shin Gam-gu, Principal
Apsan High School
Hyoji-dong, Dong-Gu
Daegu 748-962
Tel: 053-987-6543

University Schools and Departments

Undergraduate | 학부

College of Humanities 인문대학
College of Nursing 간호대학
College of Social Sciences 사회과학대학
College of Pharmacy 약학대학
College of Natural Sciences 자연과학대학
Teachers' College 사범대학
Global Leaders School 글로벌인재학부
College of IT Engineering IT 공학부
College of Economics and Business Administration 경상대학
College of Law 법과대학
College of Engineering 공과대학
Faculty of Liberal Education 기초교육원
Undeclared Major 자율전공
College of Agriculture and Life Sciences 농업생명과학대학
College of Science and Technology 과학기술대학
College of Veterinary Medicine 수의과대학
College of Music and Visual Arts 예술대학
School of Health and Welfare 보건복지학부
College of Human Ecology 생활과학대학

Graduate | 대학원

General Graduate School 일반대학원
School of Medicine 의학전문대학원
School of Dentistry 치의학전문대학원
Law School 법학전문대학원
Graduate School of Education 교육대학원
Graduate School of International Studies 국제대학원

Job Departments and Office Positions

Accounting Department 회계부
Customer Service Department 고객관리부
Finance Department 재무과
General Affairs Department 총무부
Human Resources (Personnel) Department 인사부
International Liaison Department 해외섭외부
International Publicity Department 해외홍보부
Legal Affairs Department 법무부
Marketing Department 마케팅부
Materials Department 자재부
Planning Department 기획부
Public Relations Department 홍보부
Research and Development Department (R&D) 연구개발부
Sales and Distribution Department 판매유통부
Sales Department 영업부
Secretariat 비서실, (국제 조직의) 사무국

Chief Executive Officer (CEO) 최고경영자
Chairman 회장
President 사장
Vice President 부사장
Managing Director 상무이사
Director 이사
General Manager 부장, 지배인
Supervisor 실장
Manager 과장
Deputy Manager 차장
Assistant Manager 대리
Section Chief 계장
A new employee 신입사원

Interview Questions and Answers (1) Unit 5, page 45

Here are answers for the interview questions on page 45. You can use them in the role-plays.

Questions	Possible answers
1. Tell me something about yourself.	This is often the first question. Speak about what you are good at, what you have achieved, what you hope to do, etc.
2. How would you describe yourself? This is similar to question 1, but it is about your personality. Be positive.	• I like meeting and working with other people. • I'm a perfectionist. I like to do things as well as I can. • I like asking questions and solving puzzles. • I'm very organized. I like to make plans. • I don't have any fixed ideas. I like to have an open mind. • My motto is 'Healthy body, healthy mind.' I exercise regularly and stay fit. This helps me to work well.
3. Tell me about your education. Show that you were active in many ways.	• I studied in .... College/University. • As well as studying hard, I joined the .... club. • I developed my people skills to get an all-round education. • I worked hard and won a scholarship. • I was an active member of the .... club.
4. How did you choose your college/university? Show that you are interested in many things.	• I wanted an education that covered many fields. • I chose my university because it is looking to the future. • The university/college had a strong school of arts/sciences/ medicine/education/engineering. • I wanted to study with the best teachers.
5. How do you prepare for tests or exams? Show that you work regularly. You are good at preparing for deadlines.	• I am a very organized person. • I make notes in class and review the lessons each week. • I work steadily throughout the semester. • I am a member of a study group. We review the lessons together.
6. Who was your best teacher? Why? You understand what makes a good teacher.	• I learned most from ... • She taught me about responsibility and time management. • Professor Kim was a great teacher. • ... was passionate and her classes were interesting. • I learned about project work and teamwork from ... • My supervisor was a great help.

Interview Questions and Answers (2) Unit 5, page 45

Questions	Possible answers
7. What is your greatest strength? You are confident about your abilities but not over-confident.	• I'm organized and hard working. • I plan my week so that I don't have to be in a rush. • I like to think out of the box. • I am a team worker. • I like solving problems. • I never give up.
8. What is your greatest weakness? Your weaknesses are positive!	• I want to do things perfectly. • I don't like doing the same thing every day. • I check things many times. • I spend a lot of time preparing. • Sometimes I try to do too much.
9. Describe your work or study style. You are organized and regular.	• I concentrate easily. • I study regularly without rushing. • I usually study alone or sometimes in study groups. • I take short breaks for stretching.
10. How do you manage stress and pressure? You are calm and hard working.	• Stress often helps me to do a good job. • I like being challenged and meeting a deadline. • I exercise regularly. This helps to reduce stress. • I stay calm under pressure. • Stress does not bother me much.
11. Are you a motivated person? You are very positive!	• Having a challenge motivates me. • I am motivated to do my best. • I want to do my best, for myself, and for everyone. • I love setting goals and achieving them on time.
12. What are you passionate about? You are passionate about life and work.	• I love helping people solve their problems. • I'm passionate about my hobby. • I want to make a difference. • I want the world to be a better place. • I want to love my work.
13. What makes you angry?	• I don't get angry easily. • I try to understand people instead of getting angry. • If something is not going well, I think about it.

Interview Questions and Answers (3) Unit 5, page 45

Questions	Possible answers
14. Are you a team player?	• I am happy to work alone and in a team. • Yes. I work well with others. • I was on the basketball team in school. This taught me about effort and teamwork.
15. What have you learned from your mistakes?	• I have learned many things from my mistakes. • I have learned to keep going. I never give up. • I have learned to understand other people. • I've learned to have an open mind.
16. How has university life prepared you for a career?	• University has helped my social skills. • University has taught me about myself. • It helped me to develop my talents and my abilities. • University taught me about effort and teamwork. • I learned to manage my time and mix work and play.
17. Why did you apply for this job/position/internship/scholarship? The position will give you a chance to use your talents.	• This is a great opportunity. • This position is just right for my abilities. • I want to be a member of a really good team. • This position suits my interests and passions. • I believe that I can contribute to your team. • I like the motto and the spirit of your company.
18. Why are you the best person for this job/position/internship?	• I will do my utmost for the company/school. • I work well and regularly. • You can trust me to do a good job. • My motto is 'excellence in all things.' • I can promise that I will bring excellence to this position.
19. What do you know about this job/company/school? Find out everything you can.	• The website is very impressive. • I was impressed with the mission of the company/school. • I have learned all I could about the school/company. • I like the forward-looking attitude. • I read all the brochures and studied the website.
20. What are your goals for the next 5/10/15 years? You intend to keep learning and improving.	• I want to keep learning as much as I can. • I want to develop myself personally and professionally. • I will keep learning about new ideas. • I intend to do my best for the company and myself. • It's important to keep moving forward.

Language Workshop: Three Types of Verbs Unit 5, page 46

Type 1: verb + to + infinitive complement

aim	We aim to please you.	manage	He managed to escape.
agree	I agree to marry you.	mean	I didn't mean to say that.
appear	You appear to be lost.	need	You need to stay warm.
arrange	I arranged to meet them.	offer	She offered to buy it.
ask	I asked to go along.	plan	We plan to move house.
beg	I begged to go too.	prepare	I am prepared to listen.
care	I don't care to go there.	pretend	He pretended to be asleep.
choose	I choose to walk to school.	promise	I promise to give it to you.
claim	He claims to be smart.	refuse	They refuse to come.
decide	He decided to leave.	seem	He seems to be Irish.
demand	They demanded to see him.	swear	I swear to tell the truth.
desire	She desires to sleep now.	volunteer	He volunteered to help.
expect	I expect to pass the test.	wait	I am waiting to get tickets.
fail	I failed to catch the train.	want	I want to sit down.
hope	I hope to meet you again.	wish	They wish to see her.
learn	She learned to drive.		

Type 2: verb + gerundive complement

admit	He admitted taking the cookie.	imagine	Can you imagine living forever?
advise	I advise going home at once.	keep	I keep thinking about you.
consider	Consider taking a taxi.	mention	She mentioned seeing a ghost.
delay	Don't delay making your decision.	mind (object to)	Do you mind opening the door?
deny	I don't deny being angry.	miss	We miss eating kimchi.
discuss	They discussed going to India.	practice	He practiced saying his lines.
dislike	She dislikes watching horror movies.	quit	Have you quit smoking yet?
enjoy	He enjoys playing soccer.	recommend	I recommend taking Spanish.
escape	They escaped drowning in the sea.	resume	You can resume speaking.
like	I like playing the flute.	risk	He risked losing everything.
finish	Finish writing your essay.	stop	They stopped reading.
go	They go skating every winter.	suggest	We suggest being careful.

Type 3: verb + infinitive or gerund

begin	I began to listen.	I began listening.
cease	The wheels ceased to turn.	The wheels ceased turning.
continue	She continued to watch the movie.	She continued watching the movie.
forget	I forgot to phone her.	I forgot phoning her.
hate	He hates to see her cry.	He hates seeing her cry.
like	George likes to read.	George likes reading.
love	We love to climb the mountain.	We love climbing the mountain.
prefer	He prefers to listen to jazz.	He prefers listening to jazz.
propose	I propose to invite everyone.	I propose inviting everyone.
regret	I regret to tell you this.	I regret telling you this.
remember	Can you remember to turn off the light?	Can you remember turning off the light?
start	They started to make plans.	They started making plans.
try	Try to lift the box.	Try lifting the box.

Campus Friends: Traveling Unit 6, page 52

Track 27

Here is an extra "Campus Friends" dialog, in which Emily tells Chang-min that she wants to look around Korea. Read and perform this dialog. Check the Glossary (▶ pages 147-154) for any unfamiliar words.

Emily:	Hello, Chang-min. How are things?
Chang-min:	Hi, Emily. Not too bad. How about you?
Emily:	I'd like to go on a trip this weekend.
Chang-min:	That's a good idea. Anywhere special?
Emily:	I haven't decided yet. What do you suggest?
Chang-min:	Well, this time of year, Mt. Seoraksan is always beautiful.
Emily:	I thought I'd go there in October. Anywhere else?
Chang-min:	Sure. Have you heard of Jusanji reservoir?
Emily:	Isn't that where they made the movie "Spring, Summer, Fall, Winter... and Spring"?
Chang-min:	That's right. It's the oldest man-made lake in Korea.
Emily:	I'd like to see that. Is it far?
Chang-min:	Not too far. It's in Gyeongsangbuk-do Province, in Juwangsan National Park.
Emily:	Great. I can see the lake and the mountain.
Chang-min:	Can I come with you? I haven't been there for ages.
Emily:	Of course. Let's go and find out about bus tickets.

*Information about Korean tourist attractions can be found at www.visitkorea.or.kr.

Campus Friends: Healing the World

Track 28

Ji-won and Minghua are talking about what they can do to make a difference. Read and perform the dialog together. Check any unfamiliar words in the Glossary (▶ pages 147-154).

Ji-won:	Hello, Minghua. What's on your mind?
Minghua:	Hi, Ji-won. I saw a movie last night and it made me think.
Ji-won:	Was that the one about healing the world?
Minghua:	Yes. I'm wondering how I can make a difference.
Ji-won:	How about doing the 'Three Rs'?
Minghua:	You mean Reduce, Reuse, and Recycle?
Ji-won:	Yes, that's right.
Minghua:	That's a good way to start.
Ji-won:	How about using the stairs instead of the elevator?
Minghua:	Good idea. I was thinking of getting a bicycle as well.
Ji-won:	Great. Then you will have two doctors.
Minghua:	What do you mean?
Ji-won:	Your left leg and your right leg! Cycling is very healthy.
Minghua:	Right. I'd be killing two birds with one stone.
Ji-won:	Do you really think we can make a difference?
Minghua:	Sure. Little things add up. It's important to make a start.
Ji-won:	Come on then. Let's walk to the coffee shop!

Personal Statement: Kadi Saar Unit 6, page 56

Track 29

Application forms often ask for a 'personal statement' (▶page 56). Here is Kadi Saar's personal statement. It is based on her biodata (▶page 125). Kadi is applying to graduate school.

Write about your background.

Write about your qualities.

Write about your personality.

Write about special experiences. What did you learn from them?

When did you decide on your major?

I was born in Tallin, the capital of Estonia and I went to school at the Tallin Gymnasium. While there, I played the part of Cordelia in Shakespeare's *King Lear*, and I learned to play the violin. Acting and learning the violin taught me self-discipline and diligence. They also helped me to think about art and the meaning of life.

When I was 15, I saw a road accident and this changed my life. The medics who took care of everyone impressed me and I decided to be like them. I studied First Aid and helped medics at sporting events.

What makes you different from other people?

After graduating from the Gymnasium I worked in a pharmacy and learned about medicine. I was also interested in Asian cultures, so I decided to study oriental medicine. I knew that it would not be easy, but my motto is 'Where there's a will, there's a way.' I am always ready to take on a challenge and to see it through to the end.

What ideas are important to you?

I am especially interested in both acupuncture and herbal medicine, so I am learning Chinese characters. I want to read old books about oriental medicine.

Write about your ideas.

Write about your goals.

My goal is to return to Estonia and start my own clinic. I believe that oriental medicine can help East European people through its different approach to health. I hope that you will give me an opportunity to join your school, so that I can achieve my dream of helping people to help themselves. (242 words)

Senior Advice to Freshmen Unit 7, page 64

- Here the advice given to Minghua on page 64.
- Use this advice to make your role-plays.

The exchange student program broadens your point of view.

Reading books is very important.
I wish I had read more books as a freshman.

Enjoy your life! You cannot be a freshman again next year.

Do what others do and do what you want to do. Be brave and jump in!

When you are given a chance to do something, just do it.

I recommend you to go abroad and experience as much as you can.

Read lots of books in different fields.

Figure out who you are and have lots of experiences.

My experience travelling around the world is beyond anything else in my life.

Read the conservative and liberal news journals, to get a balanced viewpoint.

Play and enjoy the life of university as much as you want now, but do not let your grades go down.

Study hard from the freshmen year and be an active learner.

Language Workshop: Relative Clauses Unit 7, page 66

1. **Relative clauses** use the relative pronouns, *who*, *whom*, *which*, and *that*:

who	people	I wish to talk with the person **who** deals with applications.
which	animals and things	I hope you received my résumé, **which** I sent last week.
which	refers to a whole sentence	I have attached my diplomas, **which** are required according to the job announcement. (▶ page 67)
whose	belonging to people, animals, and things	I have included a letter of reference from my professor, **whose** major is textile design.
whom	object pronoun for people	I was invited to apply by the company representative, **whom** I met at the job fair.
that	people, animals and things	I hope to get a job **that** is related to my major.

2. **Relative Adverbs**: when, where, why. These can be used instead of relative pronouns.

when	refers to a time expression	Do you know **when** the interview will start?
where	refers to a place	This is the place **where** Mozart was born.
why	refers to a reason	Do you know **why** I called you?

3. **Defining relative clauses** give information about a noun:

- I am the kind of person **who** would fit in well with your company. (▶ page 67)

Giving information about the noun "person"

Giving information about "My personality"

- My personality, **which** is calm and friendly, helps me to work with people. (▶ page 65)
- A nurse is someone **who** looks after sick people.

Giving information about the noun "nurse"

Giving information about the noun "people"

- Find the people who asked the same SET of questions as you. (▶ page 74)

4. **How to make relative clauses even shorter**. The relative pronouns *who*, *which*, and *that* can be replaced with a participle.

- I can talk with clients who live around the world.
- I can talk with clients living around the world. (▶ page 65)

- The man who is waiting outside has come for an interview.
- The man waiting outside has come for an interview.

- The conference, which was scheduled to take place tomorrow, has been cancelled.
- The conference scheduled to take place tomorrow has been cancelled.

Email Cover Letter Unit 7, page 67

To: personel@atlantic.com

Subject: Application for internship with Atlantic Engineering: Zhang

Attach a file | Receipt On Read : | Receipt On Delivery :

Cc | Bcc | Signature | Addresses | Save Draft | Send | Check Spelling

Internship Application Reference Number: XYZ123456

Dear Ms. Janice Spoonby,

Please find attached my application form, résumé, and certificates, which are required according to the job announcement on the website of your company.

I am applying for this internship because I think I am the kind of person who would fit in well with your company. I have an outgoing personality and experience of working with people.

I recently graduated with a degree in International Trade from Kyungpook National University, where I was a member of the university basketball team. My philosophy, which is that hard work brings success, will help me contribute to Atlantic Engineering as an active member of the Marketing Department.

During my time in university, I participated in various student clubs and studied English, Korean, and Japanese, in addition to my mother tongue (Chinese). These activities have helped me prepare for a career in marketing.

I would welcome an opportunity to talk with you about my application. My goal is to study for an MBA and an internship in your company would be a great start.

Thank you for your time.

Yours sincerely,

Minghua Zhang

757 Chong-ro
Dongseo-gu 135, Nam-dong
Daegu 704-789
053-987-6543; mzhang@hmail.com

Application-Zhang.pdf
Resume-Zhang.pdf

1. Email address as on the application information
2. Subject: Simple and relevant
3. Reference number
4. Contact person (as on the application information)
5. Email contents
6. Reason for applying
7. Short personal statement
8. Activities and experience
9. Asking for an interview
10. Closing, thanks, and farewell.
11. Contact information
12. Attached files: pdf

Story-based Cover Letter Unit 7, page 67

Track 30

Emily is applying to a tour company. She wants to guide foreign visitors to Korea during the summer vacation. She can speak to them in English and she can use her knowledge of Korean culture and history. Take a look at her story-based cover letter.

To: International Tours Ltd,
52 Dongbuk-Gil, Seo-Gu
Seoul 110-964

From: Emily Stounton
KNU Dormitory A, 305
Daegu 702-777
010-234-5678

April 21, 2013

Re: Summer tour guide – international visitors

Dear Sir/Madam,

I am replying to the advertisement for an international tour guide, posted in the Seoul-Mate magazine this April.

I have always been interested in travel and in oriental culture, and this is the reason I came to Korea. I am currently studying Asian Studies in Kyungpook National University and I think I would be a suitable person for guiding international visitors around Korea.

Even as a child I had a passion for travel and a curiosity for other cultures. I loved looking at the atlas and reading folk stories from other countries. I used to collect stamps from around the world and imagined visiting the various countries. Asian Studies first interested me in Grammar School and since then I have wanted to learn more and more. Instead of studying in the UK, I decided to come to Korea, so that I could learn all about Korean history and culture.

My passionate interest in traditions, customs, and historical figures, will make me a good tour guide, and I will be able to speak to the visitors in English. Whatever country they come from, most international visitors can speak English and I will be able to share my love of Korea with them.

My résumé and application form are enclosed, and I would be grateful for the chance to have an interview at a time and date that suits you.

Thank you in advance for your consideration.

Yours sincerely,

Emily Stounton

Emily Stounton

Unit 9: Extra Role-plays (1) Unit 9, page 86

Groups

- Here is another role-play.
- Talk to each other in your roles.
- Explain your opinions and listen to each others' opinions.
- Have a discussion about the situation.
- Make a decision together.

The new road — Role A: Politician

Situation: An expressway is going to be built from Seoul to Pyongyang. You are a politician. You think that the road is a wonderful idea. It will allow trade and tourism between North and South. People will even be able to drive to North Korea.

The new road — Role B: Farmer

Situation: An expressway is going to be built from Seoul to Pyongyang. You are a farmer. The road will go through your farm, which you must sell to the government. Your family has lived here for centuries and you don't want to sell your farm. You are very happy working and earning a little. You don't want to move, even if it means getting lots of money for the farm.

The new road — Role C: Citizen

Situation: An expressway is going to be built from Seoul to Pyongyang. You are a South Korean citizen. You don't like the idea of a new road. This will allow North Koreans to come to the south and work for low wages, taking the jobs of South Korean citizens.

The new road — Role D: Business person

Situation: An expressway is going to be built from Seoul to Pyongyang. You are a business person. You really like the idea of a road to Pyongyang. You want to be one of the first South Korean businesses in North Korea, so you can get the best contracts.

Unit 9: Extra Role-plays (2) Unit 9, page 86

Groups

- Here is another role-play.
- Talk to each other in your role.
- Explain your opinion and listen to the others' opinions.
- Have a discussion about the situation.
- Make a decision together.

Serving abroad

Role A: Young person

Situation: You have volunteered to go to a Middle East country as a non-combat soldier. You will guard hospitals and public buildings. It will be dangerous, because of terrorists, but this is a good chance to see another culture and to earn some money. You won't be fighting, so you think it should be OK.

Serving abroad

Role B: Mother

Situation: Your son has volunteered to go to a Middle East country as a non-combat soldier. He will guard hospitals and public buildings. Even though the fighting is over, it will be very dangerous, because of terrorists. What will happen if he gets killed? Try to persuade him not to go.

Serving abroad

Role C: Father

Situation: Your son has volunteered to go to a Middle East country as a non-combat soldier. You are very happy that he will be representing his country abroad. You are not worried about danger. He will be guarding hospitals and schools. He will not be fighting. He will be helping Korean companies to get contracts in the Middle East country. This will be good for Korea.

Serving abroad

Role D: Sister

Situation: Your brother has volunteered to go to a Middle East country as a non-combat soldier. He will guard hospitals and public buildings. You don't want him to go to the Middle East. You think he should stay in Korea and get a good job. Why should he be a guard in that country? Korea didn't start the war. Let the other countries clean it up.

Unit 9: Extra Role-plays (3) Unit 9, page 86

Oil in Mokpo — Role A: Fisherman

Situation: Oil has been discovered under the seabed, near Mokpo. You are a fisherman. Your family has been fishing from Mokpo for generations. This is your life. You don't want an oilrig to be built. There will be oil pollution, and the oil-company buildings will destroy the lifestyle of Mokpo. There will be no more peace.

1. Talk with the others about the oil well.
2. Explain your opinion and listen to the others' opinions.
3. Have a discussion about the situation. Make a decision together.

Oil in Mokpo — Role B: Business person

Situation: Oil has been discovered under the seabed, near Mokpo. You are a business person. Your company wants to build an oil well offshore. It will also give lots of jobs to people who live in Mokpo. Many apartments will be built. More people will come to live in Mokpo. It will be very good for the economy.

1. Talk with the others about the oil well.
2. Explain your opinion and listen to the others' opinions.
3. Have a discussion about the situation. Make a decision together.

Oil in Mokpo — Role C: Restaurant owner

Situation: Oil has been discovered under the seabed, near Mokpo. You are a restaurant owner. You are excited about the oil company coming to Mokpo. You will have many regular customers. Many new apartments will be built.

1. Talk with the others about the oil well.
2. Explain your opinion and listen to the others' opinions.
3. Have a discussion about the situation. Make a decision together.

Oil in Mokpo — Role D: Conservationist

Situation: Oil has been discovered under the seabed, near Mokpo. You are a conservationist. You don't want the oil well to be built. This will mean oil tankers and oil pollution. You want to save the wildlife. You want to preserve the beauty of the coast. Oil is causing the greenhouse effect (global warming). We must make recyclable, safe fuel.

1. Talk with the others about the oil well.
2. Explain your opinion and listen to the others' opinions.
3. Have a discussion about the situation. Make a decision together.

Unit 9: Finish the Story Unit 9, page 88

The Unicorn (England)

	The man went out of the house. The Unicorn had gone.
	The wife rang the psychiatrist: "Come quickly. My husband is crazy."
	One day, a man looked out of the window. He saw a Unicorn eating a lily.
	The man said: "Don't be silly. The Unicorn is a mythical beast."
	The psychiatrist arrived and asked the man: "Did you see a Unicorn eating a lily?"
	"He says that he saw a Unicorn eating a lily."
	He told his wife. She said "Don't be silly. The Unicorn is a mythical beast."
	(our ending)

The Favorite Dog (Russia)

	The dog used to guard the house when the man was away.
	The dog killed one wolf, and the others ran away.
	A man had a favorite dog.
	One day wolves attacked the house when the man was away.
	When the man returned, he saw the blood and the dog ....
	The dog defended the child, though there were many wolves.
	The dog was devoted to the man and his infant son.
	(our ending)

The Party (Israel)

	It was the custom for guests to each take a bottle of wine to parties.
	One man decided to take a bottle of water instead of wine.
	Once upon a time, a father gave a party for his daughter's wedding.
	However, that night ...
	He invited everyone in the village to come along.
	When they arrived, they would empty their bottles of wine into a large vat.
	He said: "No-one will notice the water, since the vat will be full of wine."
	(our ending)

Work-related Proverbs

Here are some proverbs. You can use these in your autobiography (▶ Unit 4), your personal statement (▶ Unit 6) and in your interview (▶ Unit 5). Proverbs are useful tools that can be used on many occasions.

1. Choose work that matches your values.
2. Do good and don't look back.
3. Don't leave till tomorrow what you can do today.
4. Every cloud has a silver lining.
5. Every long journey begins with a small step.
6. Failure is not falling down, but refusing to get up.
7. Happiness comes from hard work.
8. Heaven helps those who help themselves.
9. If a job's worth doing, it's worth doing well.
10. If at first you don't succeed, try, try, try again.
11. Learn from your mistakes then move on with your life.
12. Learn wisdom by the mistakes of others.
13. Little drops of water make the mighty ocean.
14. Many hands make light work.
15. Nothing ventured, nothing gained.
16. Slow and steady wins the race.
17. Smile. It costs nothing and is beyond price.
18. Some people dream of success, while others wake up and work hard at it.
19. Success is a ladder you cannot climb with your hands in your pockets.
20. The only place where success comes before work is in the dictionary.
21. To talk much and arrive nowhere is like climbing a tree to catch a fish.
22. Well begun is half done.
23. You can't solve your problems by running away from them.

Glossary

A

academic 대학의, 학술적인
accountant (공인) 회계사
accurate 정확한
achieve 성취하다, 이루다
achievement 업적, 공로
acid 산성의, 언짢은
acquire 얻다, 획득하다
action movie 액션영화
active 적극적인
activity 활동
actor 배우
acupuncture (한의학) 침
adaptable 적응할 수 있는, 융통성 있는
admire 사모하다, 찬탄하다
advertisement 광고
advice 조언, 권유, 충고
advisor 조언자
after-shave 면도 후 바르는 애프터 셰이브로션
Agony Aunt (신문 잡지 등의) 인생 상담 여성 회답자
agree with 동의하다
all in all 대체로, 총계해서
allotted time 주어진 시간
amazing 굉장한
ambitious 야심만만한, 대망을 품은, 대규모의
American Academy of Pediatrics (AAP) 미국소아과 의사협회
analysis 분석, 분석표
analyst 분석가, 분석해설자
analytical 분석적인
analyze 분석하다
anatomist 해부학자
angry 화가 난, 성난
Ankara (터키 수도) 앙카라
animal signs (출생연도) 띠
announcement 알림, 공고
anxiety 불안, 걱정, 근심
anxious 불안한
appear 나타나다, 보이다
appearance 외모
applicant 지원자, 신청자
application (취업)지원
application form 지원서
apply 지원하다
approach 접근법
appreciate 고맙게 생각하다
Aquarius (별자리) 물병자리
archery (스포츠) 양궁, 궁도
archaeologist 고고학자
architect 건축가
area code (전화) 시외 국번
argue 논쟁, 언쟁하다
argument 논리적 주장
Aries (별자리) 백양자리
arrange 정리하다, 준비하다
article (신문이나 저널) 기사
artist (painter) 화가, 예술가
assess 평가하다
assessment 평가, 진단
assignment 숙제
assistant 보조자, 조수, 점원
astrology 점성학, 점성술
astronomy 천문학
at least 적어도
atmosphere 분위기
attack (= hit) 공격하다
attitude 태도, 자세, 몸가짐
attraction 매력, 인기거리,
attractive 매력적인
Au revoir! 안녕, 또 봐요
autobiography 자서전
autumn 가을

B

Bachelor of Science (B.Sc.) (학부 졸업 학위) 이학사
background 배경, 배후
barber 이발사
behavior 행동
beliefs 믿음
bicycle (= bike) 자전거
bio 인물 소개, 약력
biochemist 생화학자
biographical 전기적인
biomedical engineer 생물의학공학자
biophysicist 생물 물리학자
board game 보드 게임
bodily intelligence 신체지능
body language 보디 랭귀지
book a room 방을 예약하다
bored 지루하게 느끼는
boring 지루한, 싫증나는
bossy 으스대는
botanist 식물학자
brainstorm 브레인스토밍하다
bribe 뇌물, 뇌물을 주다
bribery 뇌물수수행위
brilliant 훌륭한, 찬란하게 빛나는, 두뇌가 뛰어난
broadband (통신) 광대역의
broadcast 방송, 방송하다
broaden (견문 등을) 넓히다
brochure 브로슈어, 소책자
browse 이것저것 구경하다
bulleted list (보기 쉽도록) 점으로 찍어 나열한 목록
bully 약한 자를 못살게 구는 사람
business reporter 비즈니스 보도 기자
by hand 손으로
by oneself 혼자, 홀로

C

calendar 달력
calm personality 차분한 성격
campaign 캠페인
campus (대학) 캠퍼스
Cancer (별자리) 게자리
capital letters 대문자
Capricorn (별자리) 염소자리
car crash 자동차 충돌사고
career (일생의) 직업, 생애

careful 조심스러운, 신중한
caring 신경 써 주는
carpool 카풀 (출퇴근 시 자가용차의 합승 이용)
cause and effect 원인과 결과
cell phone 휴대전화
character 인물, 성격
characteristic 특성, 특징
charity 자선, 자선단체
chart 도표, 차트
checklist 체크리스트, 점검표
cheerful 기운찬, 기분 좋은
chef 요리사
chemical (명사) 화학물질
chemistry 화학
chess 체스(경기)
Chinese characters 한자
chubby 토실토실, 오동통한
citizen 시민, 국민, 주민
cleanliness 청결함, 깔끔함
clear 명백한, 맑은
clearly 똑똑히, 분명히
clever 영리한, 재치 있는
client 고객, 클라이언트
clueless 단서 없는, 무지한
cognitive 인지의, 인식의
collaboration 협력
column (표의) 칸
Come on! (재촉) 자아, (감탄사적) 무슨 소리야, 설마, 말도 안 된다
come round (= visit) 방문하다
come to life 살아나다
come true 실현되다, 이루어지다
comfortable 편안한, 안락한
comic strip 만화책
commentator (방송) 해설자
communicate 의사소통하다
communication 의사소통
compassionate 인정 많은
complete 완성하다, 완성된
completely different 현저하게 차이 나는, 완전히 다른
complex 복잡한
composer 작곡가
concentrate on (= focus on) 집중하다, 초점을 맞추다
concerned (성격) 걱정스러운

concert 콘서트, 음악회
conclusion 결론
confidence 자신감
confident 자신이 있는
confusing 헷갈리는
confused 혼란한
conscious 의식의, 의식 있는
conservative newspaper 보수경향의 신문
consider 고려하다, 생각하다
consultant 컨설턴트
consumer goods 소비자 상품
consumption 소비
contact information 연락처
contemporary 동시대의, 현대
contradictory 모순된, 반박
contribute 기여(공헌)하다
corruption 부패(행위), 타락
council 협의회, 위원회
counselor 카운슬러, 상담역
country code 국가번호
cover letter 커버 레터
cramming 벼락치기 공부
creative 창의적인, 독창적인
creative thinking 창의적 사고
creativity 창의성, 창조력
crisis 위기
criticize 비난하다, 비평하다
cultural 문화의, 문화적인
cultural understanding 문화적 이해
curiosity 호기심
current affairs 시사문제
customer 손님, 고객, 단골
CV (Curriculum Vitae) 이력서

D

dancer (직업) 무용수
data 데이터, 자료
data analysis 데이터 분석
data collection 자료 수집
deadline 마감일
debating 토론, 논쟁
debt 빚, 부채
declare 선언하다, 발표하다

delicious 맛이 좋은
delivery 전달, 이야기투
dental assistant 치과보조원
dentistry 치과학, 치과의술
dependable 믿을 수 있는
deposit 예금하다, 보증금
describe 묘사하다
desert 사막, 버리다
desperate 필사적인
destination 목적지
detail 세부사항
develop 개발하다
devious 우회하는
devoted 헌신적인
dialog 대화
dictionary 사전
difficult 어려운, 난해한
diligence 부지런함, 근면
diligent 부지런한, 성실한
diploma 학위 수여증, 졸업증서,
diplomat 외교관
direction 방향, 지시, 설명
director (영화) 감독
disagree 의견이 다르다
disallow (the referee disallowed the goal) (심판이 골을) 인정하지 않다
disc jockey (DJ) 디스크 자키
discover 발견하다
discuss 토론, 논의하다
disease 질병
distrust 불신(하다)
diversity 다양성
documentary 다큐멘터리, 기록 영화, (TV의) 기록물
domestic 국내의
dos and don'ts 지켜야 할 사항들이나 규칙
draft (first draft, final draft) 원고 (초안, 최종안)
DVD 디지털 영상 디스켓
dynamic 역학의, 역동적인
dynamite 다이너마이트

E

e-mail address 이메일 주소
Earth Sciences 지구과학
eccentric 괴짜인, 보통과 다른
eco-friendly 지구환경에 친화적인, 친환경의
eco-scientist 생태학자
economics 경제학
edit 편집하다
editor 편집자
effective 효과적인
efficiently 효율적으로
effort 노력
elderly 나이가 지긋한
electronic media 전자매체
elevator 엘리베이터, 승강기
emotions 감정
employer 고용자
encourage 용기를 돋우다
enemy 적, 적군
energetic 정력적인
engage in ~에 종사하다
engineer 기술자
enough 충분한
entertainment 오락, 여흥
enthusiastic 열심인, 열성적
entrance 입구
environment 환경
environmental engineer 환경 공학자
equipment 장비, 설비, 비품
estate 토지, 사유지, 재산
excellence 우수성, 훌륭함
exchange 교환하다, 바꾸다
exchange student 교환 학생
existence (= being alive) 생존
exit 출구, (연극) 배우의 퇴장
experience 경험, 경험하다
explore 탐험하다, 연구하다
export 수출
expressway 고속도로
extended speech 긴 연설
extrovert 외향적인 사람
eye contact 시선 마주침

F

facial expression 얼굴 표정
factual 사실에 근거를 둔
fair 정당한
fair trade 공정무역
false 잘못된
familiar 익숙한
famous 유명한
fantastic 훌륭한, 환상 같은
fashion 유행
fashionable 유행하는, 멋진
feedback 반응, 의견, 피드백
figure out 이해하다
finance manager 금융 매니저
financial reporter 경제부 기자
financier 재정가, 금융업자
findings (= results) 결과물
First Aid 응급 치료(처치)
first name (given name) 이름
fitness trainer 헬스 코치
florist 화초 재배자
fluency (말이) 유창함
fold one's arms 팔짱 끼다
follow-up 후속의, 이어지는
force 강요하다
foreigner 외국인,이방인
foreword 머리말, 서문
forgetful 잘 잊는, 건망증의
forgiveness 용서
format (문단의) 형식, 포맷
fortune-teller 점쟁이
friendship 우정
frustrated 좌절된, 낙담한
full name 성명 (성+이름)
future 미래

G

gasoline 가솔린, 휘발유
Gemini (별자리) 쌍둥이자리
gender (남/녀) 성별
generation gap 세대 차이
generous 풍부한, 관대한
genius 천재
genre (책이나 영화의) 장르
geologist 지질학자
geotechnical engineer 지질공학자
gesture 제스처, 동작
global village 지구촌
good examples 모범, 본보기
goods 상품, 물품
gourmet 미식가, 미식가의
government minister 장관
grade 성적, 점수를 매기다
graduate 졸업하다, 대학원의
graduate school 대학원
grain 곡물, 낟알, 미량
Grammar School (대학 진학을 위한 영국의) 상급 중등학교
grandparent 조부모
graphics 그림이나 사진
greedy 탐욕스러운
green energy 녹색연료
green technology 녹색기술
Gregorian Calendar 그레고리력 (현행 태양력)
guest 손님, 방문객, 게스트
Gymnasium 유럽의 대학진학과정 고등학교

H

handout 인쇄물, 유인물
hard-working 근면한, 성실한
hardship 어려움, 역경
headlight (자동차) 전조등
headline 신문기사 표제, 방송 뉴스의 주요 제목
heal the world 지구를 살리다
healthcare 건강관리
healthy 건강한, 건강상 좋은
helicopter 헬리콥터 비행기
helpful 도움이 되는, 유용한
helpless 무력한, 힘없는
herbal medicine 한약
hereby (법률) 이에 의하여
heroine 여주인공, 여장부
hesitation 주저, 망설임
highlight 가장 중요한 부분
hiking 하이킹, 도보여행
homesick 향수병에 걸린

honestly 솔직히
honesty 정직함
honor 명예, 영광
hopeful 희망적인
horoscope 점성술, 별점
horror movie 공포영화
hospital 병원
human-interest (신문기사의) 인간적 흥미
humanities 인문학
hurried lifestyle 허둥지둥 살아가는 라이프스타일
hybrid car 하이브리드 자동차
hygiene 위생상태, 위생법
hypothetical 가설의

I

ideal 이상적인
idealistic 이상주의의
identity 정체성
IELTS (International English Language Testing System) 아이엘츠 국제 공인 영어 시험
ignore 무시하다
illogical 논리 없는, 비논리적
imagination 상상(력)
imagine 상상하다
immortal 불멸의
immune system 면역체계
impatient 참을 수 없는
import 수입, 수입하다
impossible 불가능한
impression (good impression, first impression) 인상 (좋은 인상, 첫 인상)
impressive 감명 깊은
improve 향상되다
indecisive 우유부단한
independent 독립적인
indicate 가리키다, 지적하다
infant (7세 미만) 유아
infinite mass (물리학) 무한 질량, 무한대의 크기
inflexible 융통성 없는
informative 유익한
influence 영향을 주다
innocent 결백한, 순진한
instrument 악기
intellectual 지적인
intelligent 머리가 좋은
interact 대화하다
interaction 상호작용, 대화
interactive 대화식의
interfering 간섭(방해)하는
international 국제적, 세계적
International Trade 무역학
internship 인턴십
interpersonal intelligence 대인 지능
interrupt (남의 이야기를) 도중에 중단시키다
interview 인터뷰, 면접
intonation 억양, 어조
intrapersonal intelligence 자아 지능
introvert 내향성의 사람
intuition 직관, 직관적 통찰
inventor 발명가
investment 투자
issue (world issue) 화제, 관심사 (세계적 관심사)

J

jealous 질투심이 많은
jigsaw piece 퍼즐 조각
job 직업 (full time = 전업, part-time = 비전업)
job advertisement 취업공고
job announcement 채용공고
job application 취업 신청
job counselor 취업 컨설턴트
job related 취업(직업) 관련
job satisfaction 직업만족도
journalism 신문잡지업
journalist 언론인
judge 판사, 심사위원
Julian Calendar 율리우스력 (그레고리력으로 대체됨)

K

keep fit 건강을 유지하다
kill two birds with one stone (속담) 일석이조
kind 친절한, 상냥한
kinesthetic intelligence 운동 지능

L

landmark 랜드마크 (대표적 건물이나 자연적 경관 등)
last minute 막판의, 막바지의
lawyer 변호사
lazy 게으른
leader 지도자, 리더
leadership 리더십, 지도력
lean back 등을 기대다
learner 학습자, 학생
learner-centered 학생 중심의
learning 배움, 학습
lecture 강의, 강연
leisure 레저, 여가
Leo (별자리) 사자자리
liberal newspaper 진보적 경향의 (신문)
Libra (별자리) 저울자리
librarian 사서, 도서관 직원
lifelong learning 평생교육
lifestyle 생활양식, 라이프스타일
lift off (로켓) 이륙순간, 발사
linguistic intelligence 언어 지능
literacy 읽고 쓰는 능력
literature 문학
litter 쓰레기
Little things add up. (속담) 티끌 모아 태산
lobster 바닷가재
local 특정 지역의, 지방의
location 장소, 위치
logical intelligence 논리 지능
lonely 외로운
lover 연인, 애인, ~애호가
lower case letters 소문자
loyal 충실한, 성실한

M

magazine 잡지
majority 대부분, 다수
make ends meet 수지균형을 맞추다
make fun of (= tease) 놀리다
making a difference 차이를 낳음, 달라짐, 효과를 냄
malaria (의학) 말라리라
manager 지배인, 부장
map maker 지도 제작자
marketer 마케팅 담당자
material 자료, 재료
mathematic intelligence 수리 지능
meaningful 의미 있는, 중요
media 미디어, 매체
medicine 의학, 약
meditate 명상하다, 숙고하다
message 메세지, 전할 내용
mind-map 마인드맵, 생각지도
Minister of Energy 에너지자원부 장관
Minister of the Economy 경제부 장관
Minister of Tourism 관광부 장관
Minister of Transport 운송부 장관
mirror 거울
misplace 잘못 두다
moody 우울한, 변덕스러운
moral 도덕적인, 윤리적
motivation 동기 부여, 열의
motor skills 운동지능
motto 모토, 좌우명
movie review 영화논평
multiply 배가하다, 곱셈하다
muscle 근육
musical intelligence 음악지능
musician 음악가
multiple intelligences 다중지능 이론
mystic 신비가, 신비주의자

N

natural resources 천연자원
naturalistic intelligence 자연 지능
necessary 필요한
neighbor 이웃
nerves (몸의) 신경
network systems analyst 네트워크시스템 분석가
neuron 신경단위, 뉴런
newspaper 신문
NGO (non-government organization) 비정부기구
nickname 별명, 닉네임
non-verbal language 비언어적 언어
'not to do' list 금지사항 목록
numeracy 수리적 사고 능력
nurse (직업) 간호사
nutrition 영양공급, 음식물

O

objective 객관적인, 목적
observer 관찰자, 참관자
obsessive 강박 관념의
offside (축구의) 오프사이드
online 온라인, 온라인으로
open mind 열린 마음
opinion 의견, 견해
opportunity 기회
optimistic 낙천적인
order 순서
organ 신체기관, 장기
organic food 무공해 자연식품, 유기농음식
organization 구성, 조직체, (UN 등의) 국제기구
organize 조직하다, 만들다
oriental 동양의
oriental animal signs 띠
oriental medicine 동양의학
original 독창적인
originality 독창성
orphanage 고아원
outgoing 사교적, 개방적인
outline 윤곽, 개요
outlining 개요 작성하기
over-consumption 과소비
over-dramatic 너무 극적인
over-population 인구과잉
over-spending 과소비
over-use 남용(하다)
overcome 극복하다
overconfident 자만하는
overseas 해외로, 해외에서
oversensitive 과민한
overview 개관, 개략
overweight 과체중

P

paradox 패러독스, 역설
paragraph (글쓰기) 문단
parent 부모, 근원, 모체
participate 참여(참가)하다
passionate 열정적인, 열렬한
passive 수동적인
patient 인내심이 강한
pattern 패턴, 도안, 문양
pause 한숨 돌림, 잠깐 멈춤
peace 평화
peaceful 평화의, 평화적인
peer-assessment 동료평가
peer edit 동료 간 원고 교정
penalize 벌칙을 적용하다, 벌하다
percent (%) 퍼센트
perfectionist 완벽주의자
perform 행하다, 공연하다
perfume 향수
permission 허락, 허가, 승인
Persia 페르시아
persistent 고집하는, 버티는
personal 개인의, 사적인
personal statement 자기소개서
personality 개성, 성격, 인물
personality test 성격테스트
personnel department 인사부
perspective (= point of view) 시각, 견지
pharmacist 약사
pharmacy 약, 약학
philosophy 철학
phone-in show 청취자 전화참여 프로그램
phrase 문구, 구절, 표현
physical therapist 물리치료사
physics 물리학

pick on 괴롭히다
pie-chart (통계) 파이 도표
pilot 비행기 조종사, 파일럿
Pisces (별자리) 물고기자리
planet 행성
planning 계획, 기획
plot 플롯, (극, 소설) 줄거리
polite 공손한
politely 공손하게, 예의 바르게
pollution 공해, 오염
portfolio pocket 포트폴리오 포켓 (글쓰기 원고 보관)
positive 긍정적인
possessive 소유욕이 강한
Post Office 우체국
posture 자세, 포즈를 잡다
poverty 가난
practical 실제의, 실용적인
practice 연습, 연습하다
prefer 선호하다
preparation 준비
prepare 준비하다
presentation 발표, 프레젠테이션
pressure 압력, 부담
pressure points 압점
price 가격, 대가
print media 인쇄매체
private spending 개인 소비
problem-solving 문제해결
process 과정
professional 전문적, 프로의, 직업의, 전문가
project 프로젝트, 연구과제
pronunciation 발음
protect (건강을) 잘 지키다
proxemics 근접학
psychiatrist 정신과 의사
psychological 심리적인
psychologist 심리학자
public transport 대중교통
punishment 처벌, 형벌
purple 자주색
purpose 목적
pushy 강력히 밀어붙이는

Q

qualifications 자격요건
quality (개인의) 자질
quality of life 생활 수준
question and answer (Q & A) 질의 응답

R

radiation (빛, 열의) 방사
rambler 나그네
range (평가기준) 지식범위
reaction 반응
reality 현실, 사실
reasoning 추론, 추리력
rebellious 반항적인, 고집 센
recommend 추천하다
recommendation 추천
record 기록, 기록하다
recover 회복하다
recruiter 신규채용 담당자
recycle 재생 이용하다
reduce 줄이다, 축소하다
reference material 참고자료
referee (지원서의) 추천인, (축구 경기의) 심판
reference 추천서
reflect 반영하다, 숙고하다
regional 지역의, 지방의
registration 등록
regularly 규칙적으로, 정기적으로, 일정하게
relationship 관계
relevant 연관된, 관련 있는
reliable 믿을 수 있는
relocation counselor (직업 이주자 혹은 이민자 등의) 현지 이사 및 적응 상담자
Renaissance man 다재다능한 만능인
renewable energy 재생가능 연료
report 보고서, 보고하다
reporter 보도기자
represent 대표하다, 나타내다
representative 대표(적인)
repress 누르다, 억제하다
required (채용공고 등에) 규정된, ~할 필요가 있는
research (학술) 연구, 조사
research and development (R&D) 연구개발(부서)
researcher 연구자
reservation 예약
reservation form 예약신청서
resource 자원, 의지수단
resourceful 책략이 풍부한
respect 존경, 존경하다
response 대답, 응답, 반응
responsible 책임감 있는
responsibility 책임
restaurant 레스토랑, 음식점
restless 침착하지 못한, 들떠 있는, 잠 못 이루는
result 결과
résumé (= CV) 이력서
retirement 퇴임, 퇴직
reverse time order 시간역순
review 복습하다, 논평
reward 상, 보상, 수여하다
rhythmic intelligence 율동 지능
ripple 잔물결, 파문
rocket 로켓
role 역할, 배역
role model 역할 모델
role play 역할 연기, 행동으로 나타내다
romantic 낭만적인
routine 판에 박힌 일상
reuse 재사용(하다)

S

Sagittarius (별자리) 궁수자리
sample 샘플
sarcastic 빈정거리는, 비꼬는, 냉소적인, 신랄한
scenery 풍경, 경치
schedule 스케줄, 일정
scholarship 장학금
science fiction movie (Sci-Fi) 공상과학 영화(= SF영화)
scientific 과학적인

scientist 과학자
Scorpio (별자리) 전갈자리
scrambled up 뒤섞여 있는
sculptor 조각가
secret 비밀
self-absorbed 여념이 없는, 자기 중심의
self-assessment 자기평가
self-enrichment 자신을 비옥하게 함
self-pity 자기 연민
self-sufficiency 자급자족
selfish 자기 본위, 이기적인
semester (학교의) 학기
sensitivity 감성, 민감도
sentence 문장
sequence 순서, 차례
senses 감각 (촉각, 시각, 후각, 청각, 미각)
sensitive (성격이) 민감한, 미묘한
service (고객에 대한) 서비스
settle 정착하다
shallow 얕은, 피상적인
sharing 함께 쓰는, 공유하는
shave 면도하다
short-list 선발 후보자 명단
short-tempered 성마른, 불끈거리는
showy 화려한, 허식 부리는
signature 서명
significant 중요한
sincere 성실한, 진실한
single 미혼의
situation 상황
sitcom (= situation comedy) 시트콤
skeptical 회의적인
slide projector 환등기
sneakers 운동화
solar panel 태양열판
soldier 군인
solitary 혼자의, 단독의
solution (문제의) 해결, 해법
space mechanic 우주정비사
spatial intelligence 공간 지능
specialist 전문가
speech rhythm 말의 리듬
speed of light 빛의 속도
spending 소비
spill the beans 비밀을 누설(폭로)하다
spiritual 정신적인, 신성한
spy movie 첩보영화
stage name (스타들의) 예명
stage play 연극
stairs 계단
star sign 별자리
statement 말, 진술, 명제
statistical 통계상의
storehouse 창고, 저장소
strategy (대화) 전략, 방법
stretching 스트레칭 운동
structure 구조, 구성, 조직
stubborn 고집 센, 완강한
student council 학생회
study group 스터디 그룹
subconscious 잠재의식(의)
subject matter (강연의) 주제
submit 제출하다
subtract 뺄셈하다, 감하다
suggest 제안하다, 권하다
suggestion 제안, 권고
suitable 적합한, 알맞은
suitably 적절하게, 알맞게
support 지지하다, 뒷받침하다, 지탱하다
surf the web 인터넷으로 여기저기 돌아다니다
surgeon 외과의사
surname (= family name, last name) 성
survey 표본조사, 설문조사
survive 살아남다, 생존하다
suspicious 의심스러운
sustain 지탱하다
sustainable 지속가능한
sustainable society (고갈 없이) 지속가능한 사회
synapses (뇌의) 시냅스 (신경세포의 자극 전달부)

T

table 표
tactile 촉각의
talent 재능
talented 재능 있는
Tallinn (에스토니아 수도) 탈린
task 일, 임무, 과제
Taurus (별자리) 황소자리
tax 세금
teamwork 팀워크
technical 전문적인, 기술적인
technician 기술자, 전문가
technology 공업(과학) 기술
teenager 10대 청소년
template 기본형판, 템플릿
tent 텐트
theater 극장, 연극
theme 테마, 주제
therapist (임상) 치료사
these days 요즈음
throw-away society 마구 쓰고 버리는 낭비사회
tighten one's belt 허리띠를 졸라 매다
time machine 타임머신
time management 시간관리
timeline 시간대별 스케줄
title 제목
'to do' list 해야 할 일 목록
to the point 연관된
TOEFL (Test of English as a Foreign Language) 토플 시험
tough 어려운, 힘든
tourist site 관광지
tradition 전통
traditional 전통적인
traffic jam 교통정체
trendy 인기 있는, 유행의
turquoise (광물) 터키석
tutor 개별지도, 튜터
type 유형

U

Ulster (아일랜드 북부에 위치한 주) 얼스터
underwater archaeologist 수중 고고학자
unemotional 감정에 움직이지 않는

unexpected 기대하지 못한
unfair 부당한
unhappy 불행한, 불운한
UNICEF (United Nations Children's Fund) 유니세프, 유엔 아동 기금
unimaginative 상상력이 없는
unlikely ~것 같지 않은
unnecessary 불필요한
unreliable 신뢰할 수 없는
upgrade 승격시키다
upper case letters 대문자
urgent 위급한

V

valuable 귀중한, 귀중품
values (도덕) 가치
variety 다양성
various 다양한, 각양각색의
vehicles 수송수단, 매개물
verbal intelligence 언어 지능
veterinarian 수의사
vibration 진동
vice versa (생략문으로) 거꾸로 해도 또한 같음
video replay (스포츠) 비디오화면 다시 보기
viewpoint 시각, 견해, 견지
Virgo (별자리) 처녀자리
visit 방문하다
visual intelligence 시각 지능
vocabulary 어휘
volume 음량, 볼륨
voluntary service 자원봉사
volunteer 지원자, 자진하다

W

warm-hearted 마음씨가 따뜻한, 온정적인
waste 쓰레기, 낭비하다
wealthy 부유한
weather 날씨
well-being 웰빙, 복지, 행복
What's new? 별 일 없죠?
What's on your mind? 무슨 생각 해요?
willow pattern (도자기 접시 등의) 버드나무 도안
wise 현명한, 지혜로운
witty 재치 있는
wonder 불가사의, 놀라움
word stress 단어 강세
worth (doing) ~할 가치 있다
wouldn't harm a fly 파리 한 마리도 안 다치게 하다

Y

yoga 요가
You're not kidding! (= You're absolutely right!) 정말 그래!

Z

zodiac sign 서양 별자리 12궁 (宮) (Aries, Taurus, Gemini, Cancer, Leo, Virgo, Libra, Scorpio, Sagittarius, Capricorn, Aquarius, Pisces)

Answer Section

Unit 1, page 5

1. Kadi has celebrated her birthday only four times. Why do you think this is?
    - Perhaps she was born on February 29th.
    - Perhaps she was too busy to celebrate her birthday.
2. Emily is three times as old as she was twelve years ago. How old is she?
    - Emily is 18 years old. Twelve years ago she was 6.
    - It is normal for European students to enter university at 18.

Unit 1, page 6

First name	Last name	Country	Hometown	Hobby
Chang-min	Lee	Korea	Daegu	playing tennis, photography
Ji-won	Moon	Korea	Gyeongju	swimming, playing guitar
Deniz	Osman	Turkey	Ankara	mountain biking, astronomy
Kadi	Saar	Estonia	Tallinn	learning languages, playing the violin
Emily	Stounton	England	Nottingham	reading, watching documentaries
Minghua	Zhang	China	Lantian	playing basketball

Unit 2, page 12

Deniz	Hello everyone. What's new?
Minghua	Hi, Deniz. We're making plans.
Deniz	You mean studying and getting good grades?
Emily	More than that. We need to develop personally.
Kadi	And we need to prepare for our future.
Chang-min	I'm thinking of applying for an internship.
Ji-won	I'd like to be an exchange student.
Minghua	If we want good jobs, our résumés must be special.
Deniz	I know what you mean.
Kadi	Employers want to know about student clubs.
Emily	Plus leadership, teamwork, and voluntary service.
Chang-min	I'm thinking of joining a study group.
Ji-won	I'm going to work on my academic English.
Kadi	I'm thinking of being a reporter on the English newspaper.
Deniz	That's a great idea. You can improve your speaking and writing.
Emily	You're right. Let's all apply to be reporters!

Answer Section

Unit 2, page 17

Education: Walton Grammar School, GCSE 'A'level examinations in Communication and Culture, and Eastern Philosophy.

Jobs: Department store clerk

Interests: Reading, watching documentaries

Clubs: University traditional music club

Skills:

Travel: Korea

Prizes:

Future: Diplomat, UN internship

Unit 3, page 27

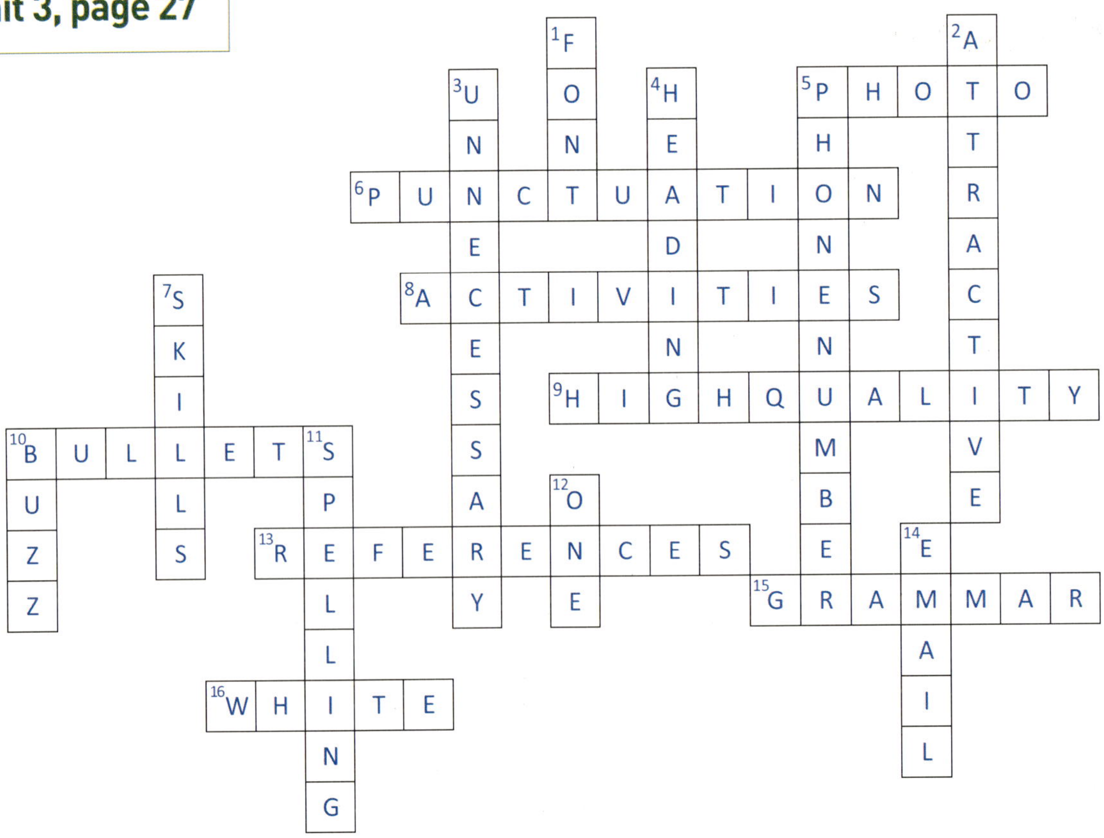

Answer Section

Unit 4, page 34

The famous Renaissance man is Leonardo di ser Piero da Vinci (April 15, 1452 – May 2, 1519) (Julian Calendar). The Julian Calendar was replaced by the Gregorian calendar in Catholic countries starting from 1582.

Unit 4, page 35

Changed name or stage name		Original name
Mother Teresa	=	Agnes Gonxha Bojaxhiu
Mark Twain	=	Samuel Langhorne Clemens
Lewis Carroll	=	Charles Lutwidge Dodgson
George Orwell	=	Eric Arthur Blair
Lenin	=	Vladimir Ilyich Ulyanov
Bill Clinton	=	William Jefferson Blythe III
Marilyn Monroe	=	Norma Jeane Mortenson
Elton John	=	Reginald Kenneth Dwight
Rain	=	Jung Ji-hoon
BoA	=	Kwon Bo-a

Unit 4, page 37

/d/	/t/	/id/	Irregular
1 saved	1 asked	1 rested	1 was
2 cleaned	2 washed	2 ended	2 led
3 lived	3 walked	3 wanted	3 understood
4 arrived	4 stopped	4 landed	4 became
5 cried	5 worked	5 lasted	5 told
6 stayed	6 watched	6 needed	6 had
loved	helped	visited	7 lost
fouled		started	8 spilt
penalized			
scored			

Answer Section

Unit 6, page 52

Emily:	Hello, Deniz.	Deniz:	Hi, Emily. Long time no see.
Emily:	I know. I went to Seoraksan last weekend.	Deniz:	You're not kidding? How was your trip?
Emily:	Fantastic. I'm traveling next weekend as well.	Deniz:	Really? You're not studying?
Emily:	I can study on the train.	Deniz:	Where are you going?
Emily:	I thought I'd try Gyeongju.	Deniz:	Great! You should visit Bulguksa and Seokguram.
Emily:	Thanks, I will.	Deniz:	Have a great time.

Unit 6, page 55

1. Our thoughts usually turn to healthy exercise, organic food **and** regular sleep. (▶ p. 53)
2. I am **not only** passionate, **but also** diligent, hard working, **and** responsible. (▶ p. 56)
3. This is causing pollution, deserts, **and** a lack of food. (▶ p. 56)
4. They told me about the need to recycle, make safe energy, **and** grow food. (▶ p. 56)
5. I am interested in **both** acupuncture **and** herbal medicine. (▶ p. 137)

Possible answers

6. In my spare time, I enjoy reading, watching movies, and meeting friends.
7. I hope to get a good job, contribute to the company, and make the most of my talents.
8. I hope not only to travel, but also to experience other cultures.
9. I hope both to be a teacher and to open my own business.
10. Every morning I either go swimming or play tennis.
11. I am applying for summer internship in either Harvard University or Stanford University.
    I am applying for a summer internship in Harvard University as well as Stanford University.
12. I prefer working in a team to working by myself.

Unit 7, page 63

Engineer, architect, pilot	Visual-spatial
Librarian, journalist	Verbal-linguistic
Accountant, scientist	Logical-mathematical
Dancer, actor	Bodily-kinesthetic
Musician, artist	Musical-rhythmic
Manager, nurse	Interpersonal
Psychologist, therapist	Intrapersonal
Florist, chef, geologist	Naturalistic

Answer Section

Unit 7, page 65

Suggested sequence for parts of a cover letter

Personnel Department
American Pacific Foodstuffs
123 Dangeun Gil, Kangbuk-gu
Seoul 010-101

Ji-won Moon
608 Moojigae APT.
Gyeongju, 780-900

April 20, 2017

Dear Sir/Madam,

With reference to your job advertisement on the asiajobs59.com website, I would like to apply for the position of assistant food advisor in your export department.

I am 24 years old and my degree, which is in food nutrition, is from Kyungpook National University. I have studied English in Indonesia and I have been an exchange student in Europe. I also have an IELTS certificate (score: 7.5).

If appointed I could communicate effectively with clients living around the world. I am single and willing to travel as part of the job.

My personality, which is calm and friendly, helps me to work with people. My motto, which I feel makes me a good applicant, is 'Cleanliness is half of health.'

While at university, I participated in the guitar club. I also received cooking certificates and taught Korean to foreigners. These activities, which I participated in regularly, have broadened my cultural understanding.

I hope to have the opportunity to talk about my application. I am free any time for an interview and I look forward to meeting you.

Thank you for your time.

Yours sincerely,

Ji-won Moon

Ji-won Moon
010-123-4567

Answer Section

Unit 7, page 66

My degree, which is in food nutrition, is from Kyungpook National University.

I graduated from Kyungpook National University where I was on the university basketball team.

These activities, which I participated in regularly, helped my cultural understanding.

My philosophy, which is that hard work brings success, will help me contribute to Atlantic Engineering.

My motto, which makes me a good applicant, is 'Cleanliness is half of health'.

The Nobel Prize in Physics for 2010 was given to Andre Geim and Konstantin Novoselov, who were professors at the University of Manchester.

Unit 8, page 76

1. "The Tree" was directed by Jimmy Wood,
2. ... based on the book by Simon Oak.
3. The main characters are played by Paul Bark, Justin Birch and Leaf Malone.
4. "Out of Time" was written by Justa Minute in 2013.
5. It is set in 2050 and 1600.
6. In the novel, a strange, backward clock is found by a young girl.
7. ... she is taken back to England in 1600.
8. Mizzo's restaurant was opened last week by the famous Italian singer, Mucho di Pasta.
9. The restaurant is located in the town center, opposite the Arts Center.
10. All the dishes on the menu are prepared by an Italian chef.
11. ... and they are brought to your table by cheerful, friendly waiters.

Unit 9, page 82

Answer Section

Unit 9, page 88

The Teacher's Jar (Korea)

3	One day, a friend came to see him. He told the students to work hard until he returned.
5	He said "Do not touch this jar. If you taste what is inside, you will die at once."
1	Once upon a time, there was a traditional Korean school.
7	As soon as he left, they began to play. One trainee suggested that they look in the jar.
2	The teacher was a greedy, stern, unkind old man with a moustache.
4	A few minutes later, he returned holding a jar.
6	A few days later, he had to leave hastily, so he told the students to do homework.
8	When they opened it, they noticed that the jar was full of honey.

Doctor Blue (Hungary)

1	Doctor Blue owned a large apartment with many rooms.
3	After the honeymoon, she gave the musician all the keys to their apartment.
5	Doctor Blue had to go to a conference, leaving the musician in the apartment.
7	Finally, he decided to look in the room his wife had told him not to.
2	She got married to a young pop musician.
6	That weekend, he looked in all the rooms except one.
4	The doctor told him he could look in any room except one.
8	When he opened the door ....
[In the original myth, the doctor was male and the room was full of his previous wives.]	

Unit 10, page 98

Chang-min:	Good morning, you two. What are you doing?
Deniz:	Hello, Chang-min. Kadi and I are working on our articles.
Kadi:	Isn't it great? We've all become reporters?
Chang-min:	Sure. What are you writing about?
Deniz:	I'm doing an article about Turkey.
Kadi:	And I'm writing about oriental medicine. How about you?
Chang-min:	I might write about the Photography Club.
Deniz:	That's a good idea. I have some photos of Turkey, as well.
Kadi:	I hope my oriental medicine article is good enough.
Chang-min:	I'm sure it will be.
Deniz:	Have you made an outline?
Kadi:	Yes, I have. I'm making my first draft now.
Deniz:	Show it to us when you finish and we'll edit it.
Chang-min:	Don't forget to have some interesting photos!

Plan of Writing Process and Assignments

Week / Unit	In class	Homework	Final step
Week 1 Unit 1	Email writing in class Final draft		→ Portfolio pocket
Week 2 Unit 2	Short bio, first draft Peer-editing in class	→ Rewriting homework (final draft)	→ Portfolio pocket
Week 3 Unit 3	Résumé, first draft Peer-editing in class	→ Rewriting homework (second draft)	→ Give to the teacher for editing, feedback
Week 4 Unit 4	Autobiography Peer-editing in class	→ Rewriting homework (final draft)	→ Portfolio pocket
Week 5 Unit 5	Teacher returns Unit 3 second draft	→ Rewriting homework (final draft)	→ Portfolio pocket
	Follow-up email Peer-editing in class	→ Rewriting homework (final draft)	→ Portfolio pocket
Week 6 Unit 6	Personal statement Peer-editing in class	→ Rewriting homework (second draft)	→ Give to the teacher for editing, feedback
Week 7 Unit 7	Cover letter, first draft Peer-editing in class	→ Rewriting homework (final draft)	→ Portfolio pocket
Week 8	Mid-term Oral Test		
	Teacher returns Unit 6 second draft	→ Rewriting homework (final draft)	→ Portfolio pocket
Week 9 Unit 8	Review, first draft Peer-editing in class	→ Rewriting homework (final draft)	→ Portfolio pocket
Week 10	Mid-term Written Test		
Week 11 Unit 9	Mini-drama project. Students plan and prepare in class. The teacher gives help and feedback where needed.		
Week 12 Unit 9	Students practice their mini-dramas in class. The mini-dramas are performed and self/peer-assessed.		→ Portfolio pocket
Week 13 Unit 10	Print-media project. Students prepare in class. The teacher gives help and feedback where needed.		
Week 14 Unit 10	Students practice their project presentations in class. The teacher gives help and feedback where needed.		→ Portfolio pocket
Week 15	Final Test: Project Presentations		